GOODBYE TO HOUNDS

GOODBYE TO HOUNDS

Christine Pullein-Thompson

Allen Junior Fiction

FIRST PUBLISHED 1952
2ND EDITION 1955
Allen revised edition 1990

To
LORRAINE
This book is
gratefully dedicated

British Library Cataloguing in Publication Data
Pullein-Thompson, Christine, *1930* –
Goodbye to hounds.
Rev. ed
I. Title
823.914

ISBN 0-85131-515-1

ONE

"One hundred and forty-four cloves. Do you really think I have to count each one?" asked my brother Laurence, standing with a recipe for mulled wine in one hand and a jar of cinnamon in the other.

"Definitely," I said, thinking how tragic it would be if the mulled wine was undrinkable on the morrow, when the Chill Valley Foxhounds would be meeting at Little Hall, our house, at eleven o'clock.

"Thank goodness Daddy's doing the final brewing," said Laurence. "At least, I shan't be completely to blame if it tastes frightful to-morrow."

I was making cheese straws. It was six o'clock on a March evening and two days to Easter. Outside, the wind was blowing across the valley. In the morning there had been a fall of snow.

Fifty cheese straws, I thought; thirty mushrooms on toast; twenty-five lobster and crab patties; six egg and ham flans cut into eight slices each; twenty-four sardine and asparagus sandwiches, and six dozen cakes; that should be enough for everyone, even if the whole of Allate—our nearest village—and dozens of East

Nightley Hunt people turn up.

"We've still got to get the beer," said Laurence.

"And dust the dining-room," I said. I put the cheese straws in the oven.

We had never had a meet at Little Hall before, even though Laurence and I and the Days, who live in a farm across the valley, founded the Chill Valley Foxhounds. At the time of which I am writing, the pack had been in existence for three years in August. Andrew, the eldest of the Days, was sixteen when it started and, having whipped-in to another pack before then, he at once became huntsman. Valentine, his eldest sister, became secretary, and Kate and I—we were then thirteen—became whippers-in later; myself first, and Kate, by choice, second. Laurence, partly because of his age—he was fifteen—but mostly because of his rather forbidding personality and his sound business head, was chosen as Master.

The Days have their own horses and Laurence and I have Overture and Daystar, which to us are the two most perfect hunters in the world.

I was thinking about Daystar and hoping that she wouldn't be too dirty on the morrow, when Laurence said, "Do you think I shall have to introduce people to one another? I've completely forgotten what one does at meets."

Laurence always panics before any social occasion concerning the hunt.

"Not unless they look left out," I said, wondering how I could possibly clean my boots, brush my hunting coat, wash my gloves, feed the horses, dust the dining-room, steam my hat, iron my hunting tie and eat dinner and still be in bed at a reasonable hour.

Then the telephone bell rang and Laurence said a word we're definitely not allowed to use, even though he's just eighteen and will be going up to Oxford in the autumn and I'm nearly seventeen, and am frantically trying to avoid being sent to further education.

"I bet it's the Days," I said. A moment later, I picked up the receiver and a voice, which I recognised as Kate's, said: "It's Sandy, isn't it? Something absolutely terrible has happened. You'll have to come down here at once—both of you. It's too awful for words. The whole house is sunk in the most indescribable gloom."

I hoped Kate was exaggerating. She generally does. I said: "Well, what's happened?" But I knew before I spoke that she wouldn't say; that she would insist that Laurence and I must hurry down to Long Chill Farm and hear the dreaded news there and discuss it for hours afterwards.

I didn't listen to her reply. I was wondering whether the meet would still be held on the morrow, whether the kennels were burnt to the gound, or Rattler had killed Vagabond, or Andrew had fallen sick and I was to hunt hounds again as I had one Boxing Day. I resigned myself to dusting the dining-room at midnight and then I said: "All right, we'll be down."

Laurence was not pleased when I told him the news.

"Why must they always be so mysterious?" he grumbled. "And why must we always go down there to hear the news? I don't suppose it's anything really dreadful, anyway. Kate always panics."

"I shall be furious if the meet's off," I said, looking at the plates around the kitchen laden with delicacies.

"We'd better take the car," said Laurence. "That is, if Daddy will let us, and collect the beer on the way."

Daddy said we could have the car, but that we weren't to be long, and if we were late we were to take our shoes off and creep upstairs, as he didn't wish to be wakened by elephantine footsteps at an unearthly hour in the morning.

Outside it was nearly dark. The air was warm in our faces, and all trace of the morning's snow had vanished.

Laurence kicked the ground. "I doubt that there'll be a frost at all tonight," he said. "There should be a wonderful scent tomorrow.

Overture and Daystar heard our voices and neighed.

"Hadn't we better feed them now?" suggested Laurence. "The Days may keep us hours and we don't want to get them up up just when they've gone to sleep."

I agreed, and while Laurence mixed Overture's and Daystar's feeds, I filled up their water buckets.

Later, Laurence collected the beer from the little cream-coloured pub beyond Allate's green and the ancient bakery, and then we drove on down into the valley.

The pond outside Long Chill Farm House was dark and shadowy. The kennel yard looked smaller in the dusk. In the stables the horses were munching.

"They must be in the house," said Laurence, glancing round the empty yards. Hounds heard his voice and started to 'sing'."

We found the Days in the dining-room, a large, friendly room, with a brick floor and an open hearth. They were sitting round the big table in the middle, apparently lost in despair.

Kate saw us first. "Oh, you're here," she cried.

Valentine looked up. She's tall and slim and, unlike most of the Days, looks her age, which was then seventeen. Andrew, who is well-built with broad shoulders and a firm, good-natured face, said: "Do sit down," which sounded strangely formal coming from someone we knew so well.

Harry, the youngest of the Days, was crying loudly in a corner. For the first time I felt alarmed. What could have happened, I wondered, to sink the Days in such despair and to silence Kate, who is usually bursting with news and wonderful plans for the future?

Laurence caught my eye and we both sat down. I noticed that the Days had been cleaning their boots; there were pots of polish and brushes lying about the room and on the dresser there was the sort of bone you use for boning boots. Perhaps Mr. or Mrs. Day has had a heart attack, I thought suddenly, and then I realised that they wouldn't have asked us down to hear that sort of news. The catastrophe must be something directly concerned with the hunt.

"Well, what is the dreadful news?" I heard my brother ask.

Andrew answered: "The farm's up for sale," he said, in a voice heavy with despair. "And Dad hasn't the money to buy it."

So that was it; and Laurence and I had always thought Long Chill Farm belonged to the Days, if we'd ever thought about it at all. They had always talked about it as "ours." "This is a boundary between *our* farm and the next." "Oh, that's *our* wood," and so on *ad infinitum*. Never had we imagined that they were only tenants; and now the worst had happened.

I realised that Kate was talking.

"It means that the kennels will go and everything," she said.

"It means the end of the hunt and goodbye to hounds," said Andrew hopelessly.

"When does your lease expire?" asked Laurence.

In six months, at exactly the same time as the auction. It's all beautifully arranged from the landlord's point of view," said Valentine bitterly. "The awful part of it is that we haven't enough money to buy another farm, even quite a small one," she continued, "and it's terribly difficult to rent one nowadays, because there are no rich landowners left to let them. It means Daddy becoming a farm bailiff or giving up altogether, either of which he'll hate."

I wasn't surprised that the Days were in such despair. They hadn't lived at Long Chill Farm for very long, but in a few years they had become terribly fond of it.

"Dad only told us this evening," Valentine continued. "Otherwise you'd have heard from us before. He's terribly cut up about it. Apparently, he had written about renewing the lease and that's the reply he got. Of course, they would have written pretty soon anyway."

"I never knew we had it on such a short lease," said Andrew miserably. "I mean, generally, you rent a farm on at least a ten or twelve year lease. They must have decided years ago that they were going to sell."

"I suppose it's the old story of death duties," said Laurence. "Who's your landlord?"

"The old Duke of Rockington was," replied Andrew, "but as you probably know, he died about six months ago. Now it's the young Duke, who lives in New Zealand. Of course, we've been given the option to buy, and at quite a reasonable price. But, apparently, there isn't a hope. It's a case of thousands and thousands."

Kate was sniffing. She had pulled her dark hair over her face. Valentine told Harry to go to bed. The fire had gone out. Through the open window there came the warm smell of spring.

I thought of the eats and the bottles of wine at home. There didn't seem much point in bothering any more about the meet now, no point in anything if there wasn't to be a Chill Valley Hunt any more. I saw long winters with no Days in the farm across the valley from home. Endless weeks with no stirring hunts to warm our blood or break the monotony of winter. It would leave an appalling gap in our life, I realised; for, though Laurence and I have always striven to avoid becoming hunting fanatics or horsy bores, the Chill Valley Foxhounds have taken a vast amount of our time and given us endless, indescribable pleasure since they came into existence.

I wondered what one did when one gave up a pack of hounds. Would we just advertise the hounds? Or would we try to find a new Master and a new hunt staff?

Andrew had risen and was kicking the smouldering logs in the fireplace. Valentine shut the window and drew the curtains.

"Surely we might be able to find other kennels," said

Laurence. "I know we can never hope to find such nice ones as the ones here. But we might be able to kennel them at a farm somewhere. Colonel Hayward might help us. Or Mr. Watson."

"But we may have to go and live somewhere quite hopeless," wailed Kate. "We may go to Sussex or Cornwall or even Scotland."

"It's all impossible. The hunt will have to give up. There's no way out," said Andrew in firm, determined accents, kicking the logs so hard that sparks flew across the room.

Laurence stood up. "Well, I'm going to think of a way out," he said, in equally determined accents. "There's always mortgages and loans."

"Dad's been into mortgages," said Valentine.

"He's been into everything," said Andrew.

"I bet he hasn't," said Laurence. "Has he seen his solicitor?"

"Oh, I expect so," said Valentine.

"And don't, for goodness' sake, start meddling," Andrew told Laurence. "You'll only make things worse."

"From what I can see they can't be worse," said Laurence. "Anyway, I'm not going to give up the hunt without a fight. If the worst comes to the worst, we'll build some kennels at Little Hall."

"And very pleased your father will be, too," said Andrew sarcastically.

"You'll have to find the money first," said Valentine. "And you won't find it in the coffers of the hunt."

"Oh, for goodness' sake don't let's quarrel," cried Kate, pushing her hair back from her face. "Things are bad enough as it is."

"We'll make it," I said, remembering an author cousin, who made sixty thousand pounds from a book. For ages I had been toying with the idea of writing; now I felt I could begin.

"We'd better get back, Sandy," Laurence said, turning to me. "We've still got an awful lot to do."

"I'll be down to fetch hounds about half-past ten in the morning. Is that okay?" I asked Andrew.

"Quite," he said.

Kate had hidden her face again. Valentine was poking the fire.

"Well, cheerio," I said.

"I shall work something out in the still watches of the night," said Laurence. "After all, we've got six months."

But the Days were beyond consolation. Kate said: "I suppose I'd better finish my boots," in miserable accents, and Andrew said: "You'll never get that fire to burn up like that, Valentine."

Laurence and I wandered out through the hall. Somewhere in a front room Mr. and Mrs. Day were listening to the radio.

"There must be some way out," said Laurence, as we reached the car. "I bet Mr. Day hasn't seen his solicitor; he's got a rotten business head. That's what's wrong with him. Fancy taking a farm on a five year lease. It's potty."

I couldn't see that Mr. Day's solicitor would be able to help him much. Laurence means to be a barrister and he seems to imagine that solicitors can help you out of any difficulty.

"Andrew's not much better," he continued. "I bet none of them have gone into the possibilities of raising a loan."

"But don't you need securities for that?" I said. "I don't believe the Days have got a bean."

It was a horrible thought and we travelled the rest of the way home in silence.

The arrangements for the meet didn't seem to matter any more and when Mummy showed me the heap of cinders which was all that remained of my fifty cheese straws, I hardly cared at all.

Laurence and I brushed and sponged and pressed our clothes without enthusiasm. We ate dinner without noticing that there was chicken and a special mushroom dish to celebrate the anniversary of our parents' wedding. We didn't bother to steam our hats or to clean our hunting whips. I dusted the dining-room and Laurence polished sixty glasses and put the table against the wall and laid the fire. In between times we told our parents the grim news and, as usual, they were consoling.

When everything we meant to do seemed done, we set the alarm clock for six, and I took two aspirins so that dreary thoughts about the future wouldn't keep me awake until the small hours. Then, with heavy hearts, we said good-night to one another and went to bed. The moon was shining through my bedroom window and outside the familiar landscape looked more beautiful than ever. In spite of the aspirins, hours seemed to pass before I fell asleep at last, to dream of a hunt which only ended with the alarm clock at six o'clock the next morning.

TWO

Hundreds of people came to the Children's Meet at Little Hall. The first of them arrived at half-past ten as I was leading Daystar out of her box before riding down to the kennels. Dozens of children arrived after that on long-coated ponies, and the vicar came on foot; and a great many women from Allate leading children by the hand and pushing prams. Mummy was still changing upstairs, and Laurence was struggling with his hunting tie.

I told the vicar to go straight in and then I hurried away down the chalky track to Long Chill Farm, hoping that I wasn't going to be late, and that Laurence would have tied his tie to his satisfaction before anyone else arrived.

It was a lovely day; warm, with a south-west wind and a grey sky. In the bustle of getting Daystar and myself ready I had forgotten the news of the night before; now it all came back to me, and in the morning light it seemed even more tragic. This time next year began to feature largely in my imagination, and I saw Long Chill Farm in different hands with electric fences stretching across the valley, dividing the rolling acres into strips and squares.

Daystar, who is fourteen-three and grey and half-Arab, was feeling fresh, and we cantered along the track when it became soft and grassy.

The Days were waiting: Andrew on his ugly brown hunter, Mulligatawny; Valentine on her chestnut, Golden Syrup; Kate on her fourteen-hand grey, Dusty; and Harry on his little pony, Lollipop. Bert Saunders, an obliging farm hand who helps sometimes in the kennels, opened the draw-yard gate and hounds came out with a rush, their sterns high and their eyes gleaming with excitement.

I shouted: "Hold up, hold up together," as Chastity and Charmer made a dash at Mrs. Day's Aylesbury ducks. Kate turned them back and I led the way across the valley towards Little Hall. We had a job to keep hounds together. They were feeling very lively and were ready to dash away in full cry at the slightest excuse. The terriers, Pick and Shovel, were lively, too. They yapped and jumped at Mulligatawny's muzzle and Andrew shouted at them, and they yapped more than ever. Dusty was in a silly mood and whenever Kate moved her whip she leapt sideways and flung her head about. When hounds had become more sensible and the terriers had stopped yapping, I said to Andrew: "It's a grand morning for scent, isn't it?" having not said one word to any of the Days beyond "good morning" since my arrival at the kennels.

His answer told me all too clearly that the Days were still in the depths of despair.

"Except for the ground being so terribly cold," he

said in the gloomiest accents. After that we rode in silence.

It was ten to eleven when we reached Little Hall. The crowd had increased considerably during my absence. A great many of our adult subscribers had arrived on foot, not liking to ride at a Children's Meet. Mr. Watson, our most ardent foot follower, had arrived and, as usual, he scrutinised us all for mistakes in tack and dress, before saying: "Hounds look very well," to Andrew, and "Your pony looks fit," to me. Soon he began to discuss the meet. "It must be costing your parents a lot of money," he said. "Wine's not cheap these days; nor's catering for that matter. Those lobster patties must have cost a lot; and prices keep rising, that's the worst of it. Did you get the White Lion to do the catering? It's very good."

I explained that Mummy and Gladys—who helps in the house in the mornings—Daddy, Laurence and myself had done the catering.

"You can cook then?" said Mr. Watson in surprised accents. "I should never have thought you could find the time."

Mrs. Simmons, the past owner of Pick and Shovel, was talking to Kate. Hounds were becoming restless. I could see Rattler watching a plate of eats being offered to the crowd. Valentine was crossing the lawn with a tray of drinks. Mr. and Mrs. Day had arrived in their landrover.

Valentine gave Andrew a drink and he gave her a message for Laurence. Harry arrived with a plate of mixed eats, and I ate a lobster patty and a slice of bacon and egg flan.

"There's a terrific crowd inside," Harry said. "The noise is simply deafening."

Valentine gave me a glass of hot wine, and I saw Daddy taking Mr. and Mrs. Day indoors.

"Andrew says Laurence is to address the children," said Valentine. "It's generally done. Do you think he'll be furious?"

Laurence and I had discussed it ages ago when the meet was first arranged. We had agreed that to talk to the children was an ordeal he could not avoid, but having reached that conclusion we had never thought about it again. Now, I knew, Laurence would be horrified. Valentine had grown tired of waiting for my answer and was on her way indoors. Willing made a dash for the house and I turned her back as she reached the front door.

The sun came out and the church clock in Allate struck eleven. I began to wonder whether Laurence and I had arranged enough draws for the day. It would be dreadful if we had drawn all the coverts blank by one o'clock and had nowhere else to go.

Daystar started to dig up the drive. My hands felt too hot in gloves and one of my boot tabs was sticking into my leg. Ludlow, the largest hound in the pack, strolled off towards the stables, and Kate pursued him, riding straight across the lawn. I wondered what Daddy would say about the hoof marks later in the day.

A reporter photographed us all, just when I was scowling and Daystar had her ears back.

Some of Mummy's smart London friends arrived and started cooing over the hounds, until True Love jumped up on a dark-haired one and left muddy marks all over her cream-coloured coat and skirt, which looked like a model from Paris. After that they all hurried indoors. The Honourable David Peterborough, a subscriber to our neighbouring pack, the East Nightley, and recently to us as well, arrived in a sumptuous, gleaming, pearl-grey car. He was dressed as impeccably as ever, though not in hunting kit. He came across and shook Andrew by the hand, and complimented him on the condition of hounds. He asked me how I was and whether I had been jumping any enormous fences lately, and he patted Daystar and said she was a grand pony. I told him to go indoors and meet my parents and have a drink. Then Valentine came out and said that the Master wished to speak a few words and would all the children come forward please, so that they could hear.

Kate and I moved hounds together and the press reporter stood ready with his camera. Laurence came out of the house and, in spite of having a scarlet coat, he seemed to look younger than ever. He fumbled with his gloves and coughed and I had an awful attack of nerves. I saw Laurence saying something ridiculous and feeling miserable for weeks afterwards, and the Days being very kind about it, but feeling furious all the same.

I couldn't bear to look at Laurence any more. I looked at the ground, and then across the road to the tall trees, and beyond them to the roofs of the stone cottages which surround Allate's green. I looked at the sky, now streaked with sunlight, and at the woods which guard our valley. Laurence started to speak: he said that he was very glad to see so many people present, and that he hoped that we would have a good day and kill a fox. Then he hesitated and, for an awful moment, I thought he was going to stick altogether. But, after what can't have been more than ten seconds, but which seemed like ten minutes to me, he continued quite sensibly. He told the field how important farmers were to the hunt; how nice they were to let us go across their land and how they helped to feed hounds by sending carcases to the kennels. He told everyone to remember always to shut gates, to avoid riding over crops, to be quiet and stand still at a check and never to press hounds. After that he thanked them all for coming and took Overture from Harry and mounted.

There was rather a feeble burst of clapping, and Laurence cried: "Hounds, please," and I led the way down the drive and out into road where shadows lay and the grass was green on the verges.

The first draw was a fir copse belonging to Mr. Smythe, a non-riding but recently pro-hunting farmer, who had been asking us to draw his coverts ever since Christmas, and who promised us a stout dog fox. The field made a great clatter along the road; there seemed to be an endless stream of ponies behind Laurence, and beyond them stretched bicyclists and cars and people on foot. I decided that it was the biggest field we had ever had with the Chill Valley Foxhounds. It would be, I thought bitterly, since it was our last hunt. The press reporter was taking photographs from the ditch. He looked vaguely familiar. I wondered whether he was from the local paper. I took the lane which would lead me to Mr. Smythe's farm. Hounds were pressing on Daystar's heels. They were ready to go at a moment's notice. I hoped that a hare wouldn't get up in front of them, or someone's pet cat.

We could see the firs now and Andrew sent me round to the far side. I found a crowd of foot followers already there. Andrew blew a toot on the horn and Daystar started to fidget. I couldn't forget that this might be the last time I should stand watching a landscape in the character of a first whipper-in and, in spite of the beauty of the day, I felt depressed. One of the foot followers, a tough young man with a military moustache, started to talk to me. He wanted to know how many hounds we had and where we would be hunting next week. I told him that this was our last meet, as the vixens had started to breed and the farmers' seeds were in. Then someone a few yards away started to holloa. I cursed the hundreds and millions of people who will talk to whippers-in when they're watching for a fox, and I searched the landscape desperately for the fox I hadn't seen. The man was still holloaing and jumping up and down with excitement.

"He came out right here," he shouted. "Just by me. He's gone back in now."

So I hadn't missed the fox after all. I felt relieved. Obviously, the man had headed him. Hounds were speaking and were quite near to us.

I said:

"Okay, I expect the huntsman's heard you," though I felt like giving a discourse on holloaing before a fox has had a chance to leave the covert.

The foot followers were all on the alert now; they stopped discussing the meat situation, 'flu and the weather, and watched the edge of the firs intently.

Hounds were near their fox judging by their cry, but every time he showed himself someone holloaed and he turned back.

Daystar became more and more impatient. Then, soon after twelve when people had started to eat their sandwiches, the fox managed to break at last. He ran down to some kale near the farmhouse, while an old farm hand, who had seen him, holloaed like mad. I galloped to the far side of the kale; the sun came out and the foot followers started to run down the hill.

It was ages before the fox broke again and when he did it was only to run back to the firs. The foot followers holloaed again and Andrew, galloping at my side, said: "He'll never run a yard with this crowd. Why can't they be quiet for a moment?"

I returned to my corner of the firs. The sun was hot on my back and I felt sleepy, and not at all like hunting. The grey sky had turned blue and a faint, warm breeze rustled among the trees. Daystar stood quietly enjoying the sunshine. Hounds were hunting well. I could see them working. Little pied Vanity picked up the line and there was a crash of music; at the same moment, I saw a big dog fox come out into the open and lope away towards a copse on a distant hilltop. I let him pass the foot followers, who fortunately had not noticed him, before I blew my whistle and, turning Daystar's head in the direction the fox had taken, I stood in my stirrups and waved my riding hat. I thought, perhaps this is the last time I shall ever stand like this and hear Andrew doubling the horn, and hear hounds, our own Chill Valley hounds, join together in a crashing burst of music as they break into the open. I could still see the fox as he reached a distant hedge and then Andrew was at my side crying: "Come on, what are you waiting for?"

Mechanically, I counted hounds and saw that they were all on—thirteen couple—so close together that they looked like one. The distant hedge wasn't wired and Mulligatawny and Daystar took it in their stride. We landed in a field of seeds and, swinging right with guilty consciences, we followed the headland to a gate, which I was about to open when Andrew cried: "We'll go over," and rode Mulligatawny at it, as though he meant to win a race. I knew he was thinking this is the last time, and not caring whether he broke the gate or his own neck. Daystar rushed rather and took off too near and rapped the top bar. Then we were galloping on uphill towards the copse.

Hounds had checked beyond the copse in a field full of cows. Andrew cast them carefully with an eye to the wind, and to osiers down by the river, which we could see now from the hilltop. The field were running away; they came galloping up the hill, and half a dozen children charged straight into hounds, who were just picking up the line. Laurence shouted: "Hold hard," and Andrew shouted: "Mind out," and then hounds were away again with a tremendous cry which echoed across the countryside.

Kate was standing near the osiers waving her cap. I realised that she had seen the fox. I yelled: "Look," to Andrew, and pointed. He answered with a nod and said: "He's gained a bit. Pity about the cows." And I knew he meant the cows had foiled the line across the last field.

We reached some rails and, though a strand of wire ran along the top bar, Andrew didn't hesitate. He rode Mulligatawny at it and was over, and, before I had time to think, Daystar was over, too, and we were galloping down towards the osiers and to Kate, still waving her cap. The river meadows were beautiful in the sunlight. Even the osier beds looked warm and almost friendly and, along the river bank, members of an angling club were fishing.

"He looks pretty tired," said Kate, when we reached her, "and they're all on except the terriers."

Andrew said nothing. He was looking beyond the osier bed across the river meadows, and, following his gaze, I saw the hunted fox. He was running more slowly and one of the anglers had seen him and was waving his arms and shouting.

Hounds came out of the osiers. They were more strung out now; Rattler was in the lead and old Vampire was some way behind.

We followed a muddy track and crossed a bridge and opened a gate which was too narrow for anyone to jump, even Andrew in his present reckless mood. We shouted thanks to the still-waving angler, I took down some wire and we forded a stream. Daystar was sticky with sweat and caked with mud. I felt much too hot in my hunting coat, my thick cream-coloured breeches, my boots, my woollen shirt and my hunting tie. I realised that somewhere I had lost my gloves. Andrew's scarlet coat was spattered with mud and Mulligatawny looked hot, but not at all tired. We couldn't see hounds any more; but we could still hear them hunting furiously in a little wood behind some tall, prosperous-looking houses. We turned towards the wood with one accord, but only to find our way barred by a stream with a wire fence on each side.

"We'll have to try the gardens," said Andrew. "With any luck, the wood belongs to one of those houses and there'll be a gate."

The field was nowhere to be seen. The sun was still shining. We rode into the garden belonging to the largest of the two houses. We rode up some steps, across a rockery and through a tennis court. We heard shouts behind us, but we didn't care because we had seen a little wicket gate giving access to the wood, and because this was probably our last hunt with the Chill Valley Foxhounds and we wanted to enjoy ourselves more than anything else in the world.

Unfortunately, by the time we reached the wood hounds had left it and, as it was wired all the way round, we had no choice but to ride back through the tennis court, over the rockery again and down the steps, at the bottom of which the owners of the house were waiting for us. They looked very cross, and Andrew raised his hat and said: "I'm very sorry to have disturbed you, sir," to the man who stood in front of us wearing jeans and carrying a golf club, and, "We haven't done any damage, madam," to the woman, who was wearing a windcheater and a tweed skirt.

I think the sight of Andrew's scarlet coat must have subdued them for a moment, because they didn't say anything until we were past, and then the man only shouted: "I'll tell the police," rather feebly and not as though he meant it.

We rode out of the garden on to an unmade road.

There were houses on each side, fenced by split oak and high hedges. We couldn't hear hounds any more and there was no chance of our seeing them unless they crossed in front of us.

Andrew cursed. "There must be some way down to the river meadows," he said. We found a way, but it was a narrow path with posts across and a notice saying *No Cyclists*. We couldn't get the horses between the posts, which were too firmly encased in concrete to be pulled up or knocked down. Andrew cursed again and we rode on.

"They'll be in the next county by now," said Andrew. "Oh, how I hate suburbs."

I said nothing. It seemed awful that our last hunt should be spoiled by wire and suburbs. I hoped that Kate was with hounds. We heard hoofs behind and, suddenly, the whole field, or rather what was left of it, came into view galloping along the rough road.

Overture neighed when she saw Daystar, and Laurence shouted: "Gosh! I'm glad to see you. Are they anywhere about?" meaning hounds.

Andrew pointed across beyond the houses. "They were over there ten minutes ago," he said. "But goodness knows where they are now."

We all rode on together and Valentine said: "Isn't it a glorious run?" And Harry shouted: "Lollipop's going beautifully and jumping absolutely everything."

We came to a large village with shops and the populace rushed to their gates and windows and doors as we clattered down the high street. We reached a bridge and Laurence said: "They won't have crossed over, will they?" meaning hounds over the river.

Andrew said: "There must be a towpath." The river was still swollen by February's rain. It gleamed in the sunlight and reflected the bridge and the willow trees beyond. Andrew found a hunting gate, and in a matter of seconds we were galloping along the towpath and, more wonderful still, we could hear hounds again, not making so much music now, but still with a wonderful cry.

Away on our left, I could see Kate galloping steadfastly across the wet river meadows. Soon, we could see hounds, and in front of them a wood, and beyond it, gravel pits still being worked.

"I shouldn't be surprised if they kill," said Andrew. "He must be pretty tired by now."

We didn't seem to be gaining on hounds at all, though Valentine, Laurence, Andrew and myself had given our horses their heads and had already outdistanced the rest of the field.

"This is the best run we've ever had," said Laurence.

"It would be, because it's the last," said Andrew.

"Not necessarily," said Laurence obstinately.

I hoped that Andrew and Laurence weren't going to quarrel. It seemed a ridiculous moment to start. Hounds were very near the wood now.

"Only time will show," said Valentine.

"Time's always against you," said Andrew.

"Look, they've reached it," I said, urging Daystar faster and pointing to where hounds were crossing a stream, before plunging into the wood.

Daystar felt tired. I hoped that hounds would check for a moment, to give her a chance to get her second wind. Overture was dark with sweat. We reached the wood, and Andrew threw me his reins, and dismounted and plunged through the stream, which was wired on each side.

Hounds had stopped hunting. The river meadows suddenly seemed very quiet. Valentine, Laurence and I dismounted and the field came up. I ate my sandwiches, which I had forgotten until this moment. They were filled with cheese and tasted very good. Hounds began to appear along the far side of the fence.

Then Andrew appeared and shouted across the stream to us: "I reckon they've killed him."

"That's fine," shouted back Laurence. "I should think it's more than likely."

Kate had arrived and we told her the news. Andrew waded back through the stream and blew hounds out. Kate and I counted them as they came and after a few minutes we found they were all on—thirteen couple of tired, happy hounds.

"I wish it had been a proper kill," said Andrew, taking Mulligatawny from me. "Do you realise we've never had one and never will now? And he may have gone to ground."

We all mounted again. Hours seemed to have passed since the meet, but, looking at my watch, I saw that it was only half-past three. Andrew blew "Home," and Laurence said: "The end of a nearly perfect day."

Andrew seemed to know the way to the kennels. We rode across endless river meadows and the afternoon turned to evening, and in all the trees birds were singing of spring. It seemed ridiculous to be miserable on such a lovely evening and I kept forgetting the catastrophe hanging over us, and whistled and sang, only to be brought back to reality by Andrew's reproachful eye.

The Haywards were still with us, Patience and Felicity on their ponies Jester and Joker, and they talked merrily. Their presence stopped us discussing the future and becoming even gloomier than the Days were already.

We came at last to a familiar road, twilight descended suddenly, and a few careful motorists already had their lights on. The horses were tired. Daystar tripped more than once, and Kate thought Dusty might be lame, though no one but she could see anything wrong. A few miles before Allate the Haywards left us and we were alone with our hunters and our hounds.

Andrew turned in his saddle then and said: "Do you realise this is the last time?" There was a choke in his voice and we all knew how miserable he was feeling. The evening seemed full of melancholy now and even the birds in the trees seemed to be singing sadly. Daystar's hoofs beat "Last time, this is the last time," on the road with tiresome monotony, and I could hear Kate sniffing behind.

"You're too defeatist," said Laurence in a voice which was supposed to be cheerful but only sounded grim.

We still hadn't the terriers and occasionally Andrew blew for them, the horn sounding loud and somehow clearer in the evening air. Shovel joined us before we reached Allate, but there was still no sign of Pick when we took the track which would lead us down into the valley and to the kennels.

It was quite dark when we saw the light of Long Chill farmhouse and farther away, half-way out of the valley, the lights of Little Hall. Andrew blew "Home," to tell Bert Saunders we were near and hounds began to hurry. Once again I thought, this is the last time, and wondered whether there would be the usual boiled eggs for tea or whether they had all been eaten at the meet.

Bert Saunders was waiting for us in the kennel yard. He asked his usual question. "Did you catch a fox?" he said, as the Days dismounted from their weary horses. It was pleasant to be able to answer "Yes," for the first time in months. Laurence and I offered to return to the kennels later and look hounds over for thorns and cuts and feed them, but Andrew said that it was all right, he and Valentine and Kate and Harry would manage beautifully, and Bert Saunders said: "The puddin's all ready in the copper. It only needs putting in the troughs."

So we said good-bye and rode back across the valley. Half-way home, Laurence said: "After our baths we must have a conference about the future of the hunt. The Days obviously are going to do nothing. It's amazing that they should be so defeatist."

"I expect Mr. and Mrs. Day are pretty gloomy," I said, "though I can't see Mr. Day giving up the farm without a fuss."

"I don't know. I think a few legal papers would be enough to defeat him," said Laurence. "Anyway, I'm going to get to work over the weekend. I'm sure there's some way round."

I hoped that Laurence was right. We settled the horses and then we had hot baths and, later, tea with boiled eggs and bread and butter and honey.

We discussed the meet for a long time and learned from our parents that all the food and wine was finished. We discussed the day's run and where we had been and each exciting moment and then, quite suddenly, I noticed that Laurence had fallen fast asleep in front of the fire with his mouth open. He wakened in time for dinner, but afterwards he fell asleep again and when he wakened for the second time at half-past nine, we both agreed that the conference on the future of the hunt must wait till morning.

THREE

I wakened on Sunday morning and knew at once that a difficult day lay ahead. Outside the sun was shining and I could hear a bird singing in the cedar tree on the lawn. It seemed sad that trouble must come with such a lovely spring; I saw sparkling April days ahead spoilt by dreary thoughts and the Days cross and despairing all through the long summer. I couldn't bear to think about the future any more, so I dressed and took my parents some tea and wakened Laurence.

I fed the horses, and then Laurence appeared, looking very sleepy, and we mucked out the boxes. After breakfast we groomed the horses and I peeled some potatoes for lunch and Laurence laid the dining-room table. Then it was time for elevenses, and we couldn't put off the conference any longer.

Laurence had hardly spoken all morning. We took our cups of Bovril into the room we still call the nursery and I switched on the electric fire and Laurence said: "I've thought of a plan." He pushed his hands through his dark hair and said: "I'm going to see the estate agent or whoever's in charge. I don't see why we shouldn't buy the kennels just on their own."

"But we haven't any money," I cried, astounded to hear such a suggestion from Laurence, who has always been particularly money-conscious.

"We can make some then," Laurence replied. "We can hold hunter trials and a hunt ball and a gymkhana, and even things like a jumble sale. We might even make enough to buy some of the stables and a bit of the field behind."

I couldn't say anything for a moment. I was surprised; it sounded too easy, and yet, all that Laurence suggested was possible, except for one thing. "But will it be any good buying them?" I asked, "if the Days go and live in Cornwall or Scotland?"

"Perhaps they won't, if we've bought the kennels," answered Laurence. But, by the way he said it, I knew I had touched the weak spot in his plans.

"But we'll have to get the Days to help," I said. "We can't run hunter trials and hunt balls without them."

"We'll have to talk them round," said Laurence. "We had better pop down this afternoon and see what we can do."

I thought about Laurence's suggestions during the rest of the morning. I didn't like the idea of a hunt ball very much, and I didn't think it a very practical suggestion either, since neither the Days, Laurence nor myself could dance and knew nothing at all about balls. The hunter trials, I thought, would be much more fun. I imagined riding the course on Daystar. I wondered where we would hold them and whether we would have a class just for the members of the Chill Valley Hunt. I felt more cheerful. Laurence might be right. If we kept the hunt going, the Days might well decide to stay in the district. I began to look forward to the weeks ahead.

After lunch, Laurence and I jogged the horses out for each other's inspection and agreed that they were both as sound as bells and hardly tucked up at all, considering the gruelling hunt they had survived the day before. Then we called Quinky, our black cocker spaniel, and walked down through the valley to Long Chill Farm.

We found the Days quarrelling in the saddle-room. Andrew was complaining, because Kate insisted on whistling a song from *Don Giovanni* completely out of tune. Valentine was furious with Harry because he hadn't looked at Lollipop since his return from hunting the day before. It was obvious that all their nerves were on edge.

Andrew saw us and said: "Oh, hallo." Kate stopped whistling. Valentine said: "Well, I think you're jolly mean and don't deserve a pony." Harry looked at Laurence, whom he secretly admires—I can't think why—and said: "You're just in beastly tempers, all of you. I can see Lollipop from my bedroom window and I know he's all right." Then he walked out of the saddle-room with his head held high.

"How are things?" asked Laurence vaguely, apparently not noticing the tactlessness of the question.

"Impossible," answered Andrew shortly.

"Worse than ever," said Valentine.

"Absolutely unbearable," said Kate with a choke in her voice, taking a bridle from a hook and looking at it.

"Did Pick turn up all right?" I asked, wishing to

change the subject.

"No, not really," said Andrew. "The Chidlington police rang up and we had to collect him from the police station. Apparently someone saw him running down the main road and took him there."

"How are the horses?" asked Laurence after a short silence. "Is Dusty all right?"

I wondered why we were making such stiff conversation. It was unusual between us and the Days.

Kate said that Dusty was all right except for slightly filled forelegs.

We wandered over to the kennels and on the way Laurence muttered in my ear: "I think we'll leave telling them to another day."

I nodded agreement.

Hounds were sunning themselves in the courts which adjoin the lodging-rooms. They looked happy and comfortably tired. They stood up and waved their sterns and smiled when they saw us approaching. Once again I thought of the approaching summer: soon there would be cheerful, smiling puppies, Chastity's, Charmer's, Wasteful's and True Love's children. We would need lots of walks for them and plenty of food. We ought to have a hound show, I thought, when they all come back. In August there would be long conditioning rides and the first cub-hunting days. There seemed so much to look forward to, if only the Days stayed near and Laurence's plans came true. I looked at the kennels and remembered the summer when we had converted them from farmyard buildings to what they were now. It had been a scorching August that year and we had all worked and sweated and quarrelled under a blazing sun. We had suffered from blisters and backache, but in the end it had been worthwhile. I thought of the next year when we had painted, improved and enlarged the kennels during term time as a surprise for Laurence, the only one of us to languish at a boarding school. It was then that we had erected the sign that stands at the end of the lane which leads to Long Chill Farm; the sign which reads, *To The Chill Valley Hunt Kennels.*

And this summer, I realised, would be the scene of the greatest struggle of all, the struggle for survival.

Well, Laurence and I are going to fight anyway, I thought, fight to the death; and with a cold feeling in the pit of my stomach, I wondered what we would do if the estate agents refused to sell the kennels separately. Certainly, Laurence seemed to have no plan but the one I knew, and I could think of no other solution to our difficulties.

Andrew and Laurence were discussing the Duke of Rockington's estates. When Laurence had an opportunity, he said: "Who are the people in charge of the selling arrangements anyway?" in an off-hand way, which only I could tell was affected.

Andrew named a firm of solicitors in London. "And some estate agents have got a finger in the pie, too," he said. "Body & Peel, Ltd. They hang out near Clifford Street. Why they didn't put a local firm in charge, who know the estate personally, I can't imagine."

"I can't imagine either," Laurence said, and then: "We had better go, Sandy. It's nearly tea-time."

The Days talked a little longer. Laurence, now having the information he sought, was impatient to leave. He cut their conversation short and soon we were hurrying along the track to home. When Laurence is excited he always walks at a tremendous pace; today was no exception and I was panting and my legs ached by the time we reached Little Hall.

"Tomorrow I shall go to London and see both the solicitors and the estate agent," he announced as we went into the dining-room for tea.

The next day I rode down to the kennels and helped Andrew shake sulphur into hounds' coats, and listened to his gloomy views on the future.

"I shall get some sort of job," he said, "if we leave here. I can't go on helping Dad on the farm when the farm doesn't exist. The worst of it is I haven't any training—university, I mean—and people always want that nowadays."

"But you've lots of experience," I said, "and people always want that."

"I shall take a job in kennels if I can't get one on a farm," Andrew continued, not seeming to notice my remark, "and become a professional huntsman."

"But perhaps everything will turn out all right," I said. "A benign millionaire may buy the estate as an investment and let the old tenants stay. You can't tell what may happen."

"You Darlingtons are hopeless optimists." grumbled Andrew. "I wish you'd face facts."

"We do," I said. "We face them all the time."

"Why's Laurence gone to London anyway?" asked Andrew suspiciously.

"To buy clothes before he goes up to Oxford," I replied, congratulating myself on my quick retort.

But Andrew wasn't taken in so easily. "But he's not

going up till the autumn," he said.

"Well, because he's sick and tired of the gloomy atmosphere around here," I replied, thinking quickly. "And he wants to go to the Academy, and to spend his Christmas book token before it's out of date."

But Andrew wasn't listening. He had lost interest in Laurence's movements. "Poor old Vampire's thin," he said. "We won't he able to draft him. We should have put him down at the end of last season, really. And Vanity, she's another one who ought to go."

By "ought to go" Andrew meant to be destroyed.

I protested: "But Vanity was hunting beautifully on Saturday," I said. "Didn't you see her pick up the line first in the firs?"

"Yes, but she was dead beat at the end," said Andrew. "It's not fair to keep them going on when they're like that. Valiant's another one who'll have to go. It's not fair to expect seventh and eighth season hounds to start life in a new pack. You must remember that they were old hounds when they came to us from the Downshire, and that was two seasons ago."

It seemed to me that Andrew meant to destroy half our pack, rather than let them go to other kennels. I looked at Vanity and I couldn't see that she looked either old or decrepit. I felt very angry with Andrew.

"Will you want to be destroyed when you're too old to hunt all day without being tired at the end?" I asked.

"I don't know. Perhaps I shall. It's possible," said Andrew.

After that, we worked in silence. I was quite glad when lunch-time came and Andrew said: "There's no point in your coming down this afternoon, Sandy.

I shall be on the tractor. Valentine's going into Chidlington about a secretarial course and Kate and Harry are going out to tea."

I saddled and bridled Daystar, who had spent the morning in one of the Days' many loose-boxes, and rode home to a lunch of eggs in cheese sauce followed by rhubarb, which I love. Andrew's remarks preyed on my mind and I felt sad all afternoon.

Laurence had said that he would be back in time for dinner, and I began to feel more cheerful after tea. I caught Daystar and Overture, who had been out in the paddock during the afternoon and fed them and put on their rugs. I helped to wash up the remains of tea and began to fry the fish for dinner. Then I heard the car horn and, dashing outside, I saw the car coming through Allate. Laurence had caught the same train as Daddy and, as they came up the drive, he put his thumbs up.

"We can buy the kennels and a piece of the field behind and the loose-boxes for five thousand, he shouted. "But the farm's still for sale, privately for two hundred thousand, or by auction on August the eighteenth."

"Two hundred thousand! No wonder the Days couldn't afford to buy, I thought. And five thousand pounds seemed a lot of money to raise by hunter trials and a hunt ball. But Laurence laughed aside my fears.

"We'll charge five pounds for each car at the hunter trials," he said, "and a lot for the entries. The hunt ball tickets can well be twenty pounds each."

"But will anyone come at that price?" I cried, hurriedly thinking that a double ticket would be forty pounds.

"Of course they will," said Laurence. "If the tickets are any cheaper, they'll think it's a scruffy affair and be put off. We'll hold it in a hotel," he continued. "Then we won't have to bother with the catering."

"The White Lion?" I asked, because we had had a farmers' dinner there.

"Not big enough," said Laurence. "We need a sumptuous ballroom. I believe there's a country club between Chidlington and Hettington that might do."

I must have looked worried because Laurence said: "Honestly, Sandy, I don't see why it shouldn't be a success. After all, there aren't any hunt balls round here. I don't believe the East Nightley's ever had one."

I still felt dubious. Five thousand pounds still seemed a lot of money to me. "It's a pity we can't sell Lost Horizon," I said, remembering the bay mare one of our subscribers had given to the hunt and which, so far, we had hardly ridden at all.

"We must get on and ride her now that hunting's over," Laurence said. "After all, she may turn out to be a wonderful jumper and win fifty-pound prizes, you never know."

I said nothing. It seemed to me that today Laurence's optimism was endless. I wished that I could feel the same.

"*Horse Breeding and Stud Management* by Henry Wynmalen," said Laurence who, I realised, was telling me about the book he had bought. "I read some of it coming down in the train. It's jolly good. I shall show it to Andrew tomorrow and see what he thinks of it."

"I hope he's in a better mood than he was today," I said.

"So do I," said Laurence. "Because tomorrow we'll have to tell them our plans."

Telling the Days our plans wasn't easy; and when Laurence and I had accomplished it, their remarks were far from encouraging.

"Ten to one it will rain and no one will come to the hunter trials," Andrew said. "And the band for the ball will cost a hundred and we won't sell more than twenty tickets."

"Five thousand pounds is an awful lot of money," Valentine said.

And Kate, who is usually so full of enthusiasm for any new enterprise, made the most depressing remark of all. "But what's the good if we're living in Cornwall?" she said.

I could see Laurence was exasperated. I must say I felt angry with the Days.

"I don't believe you care about the hunt," I cried, glaring at them each in turn and remembering that Laurence had given up a whole day to seeing solicitors and estate agents, and thinking how ungrateful they all were.

"Don't be silly," said Andrew, "of course we care."

"Well, why won't you try and help, then?" I asked angrily.

"After all," said Laurence, "even if we can't keep up the hunt, five thousand pounds will still be useful for something. We can give it to The British Field Sports Society or some other worthy cause.

"Hunter trials would certainly be fun," said Kate,

suddenly sounding more cheerful. "Would we be able to compete?"

"I don't see why not," said Andrew. "Most hunts compete in their own hunter trials."

"I suppose we'd better hold them at the end of April," said Valentine. "Before anyone's back at school."

"We haven't much time," said Andrew.

"Long enough, though," said Laurence, grinning triumphantly at me.

"We'll get to work at once," said Valentine, sounding businesslike. "I'll get a pencil and paper."

The atmosphere had cleared. It felt much lighter, like the air does when a threatened storm has died down without coming to anything. We were in the saddle-room. The Days had been cleaning their tack when Laurence and I arrived.

"Class I for subscribers and farmers of the Chill Valley Hunt," Andrew said, when Valentine returned with paper and pencil.

"Class II for members of adjacent hunts," said Valentine, scribbling furiously.

"i.e.?" asked Laurence.

"The East Nightley and ... Which are our nearest hunts?" said Andrew.

"Gosh, I don't know," said Valentine. "We'd better look up in *Baily's Hunting Directory* and see if we can find out."

"Class III for young persons under sixteen. That means I can enter," said Kate.

"Class IV, pairs, open," I said, wondering whether Daystar would go best with Dusty or Overture.

"We haven't had an ordinary open yet," said Andrew.

"Don't go so fast. I haven't written half of it down

yet," said Valentine.

"What about a class for the best three from any hunt," said Laurence. "Don't some hunter trials have that now? We could get up two threes."

"Yes, there's a special cup for it somewhere. *The Duke of Sutherland.* You have to all come from the same pack. And to have hunted regularly with it I suspect," said Andrew.

"Oh, do let's have it," cried Kate. "We could have Mulligatawny, Pink Gin and Golden Syrup together and Overture with Daystar and Dusty each on one side."

"Perhaps Lost Horizon will be able to compete if we school her seriously," said Laurence. "She's got quite a jumper's bump, you know."

"These are the classes I've got so far," said Valentine:

"Chill Valley only.

"Adjacent.

"Children.

"Open.

"Pairs.

"Threes."

"Six classes," said Laurence. "Is that too many?"

"It's rather a lot," said Andrew. "We don't want them to go on till nightfall."

"And it's not as though we can possibly ride in more than three each," said Kate. "I mean, our horses will be exhausted."

"Do you think there'll be any entries in the Chill Valley class besides ourselves?" asked Valentine.

"David Peterborough and Mr. Austin Smith and perhaps a couple of others," said Laurence.

"Why don't we join the Chill Valley and Adjacent

class together?" I suggested.

"That's an excellent idea," said andrew.

"First class in both senses," said Valentine.

"That makes five all told," said Kate. "Is that still too many?"

"We want to make lots of money," said Laurence, "and people won't come for one class. I think five's the perfect amount."

"Certainly not too many," said Andrew. "The question is, ought we to have a ladies' class and a farmers'?"

"Instead of pairs or threes?" asked Kate.

"Perhaps," said Andrew. "Of course, we may find the fences aren't wide enough for threes. Where are we going to hold it, by the way?"

"What about Melcham?" suggested Laurence. "I'm sure Colonel Hayward would let us have them there. He is so very pro the hunt. There are plenty of hedges, too, and that little hill beyond the plantation would do beautifully for the judges' wagon."

"Yes, I should think Melcham would do as well as anywhere," said Andrew, after a moment's thought. "There are plenty of rails scattered around, and, as you say, several hedges."

"And it's on a bus route, which is good from the poorer spectators' point of view," said Kate.

"I suppose we'll start about half-past nine," I said, seeing refreshment tents, flags and a distant wagon, in my imagination.

"Or ten," said Andrew. "We'll have to work out a programme. But we'd better decide the date next."

After a short discussion we chose the third Saturday in April.

"What about judges?" asked Kate.

"I don't know anyone who would do," said Andrew, after a pause. "It mustn't be a local person and it must be someone who's used to judging."

Suddenly I had a brainwave. I thought of Major Sunderland and Mr. Peterson, the joint Masters of the Waynesbury Hunt who had let us have three couple of hounds as well as Ludlow, Spendthrift and Conscript. The others were delighted with the suggestion; Valentine volunteered to write the appropriate letter as soon as we had Colonel Hayward's permission to use Melcham.

"And now what about the ball?" asked Laurence, and a long silence fell.

"I don't know anything about such things," said Andrew at last.

"Nor do I," said Laurence. "But it *is* a way of making money. Several hundreds, so I'm told."

"There's not much to it," said Valentine. "I'll get the invitation cards printed and we'll send them to absolutely everyone we know, who we think may be able to afford it. I'll send an advertisement to the Press, and we'll book a fashionable band and a disco. Where we hold it seems to be the most difficult problem at present."

Laurence told her of the Country Club between Hettington and Chidlington.

I thought how efficient was Valentine and what a wonderful secretary she would be when she was fully trained and could manage computers and type millions of words a minute.

"Will we all have to buy long dresses for the beastly thing?" asked Kate. "Because, if we have, it seems to me that they'll cost as much as we're likely to make out of the tickets."

"Not if we're clever. You can borrow and I need one anyway," said Valentine, who seemed to be looking forward to the ball.

"I don't think we'll be able to go anyway, Laurence," said Andrew, "because we haven't got the right sort of scarlet coats. Not that I shall mind stopping at home."

"But you must both be there," cried Valentine. "Laurence has got to shake everyone by the hand and Andrew's got to blow the horn when we have the gallop near the end."

I realised, suddenly, that I had been wrong in thinking that none of the Days had ever been to a hunt ball. I remembered that Valentine had stayed with an aunt in January and had gone to a ball with a cousin.

"I think we had better put you in charge, Valentine," said Laurence. "You're the only one of us who knows anything about hunt balls."

"But you've got to be there," said Valentine. "I'm not going to run it, unless you promise to receive the guests for, at least, the first half hour."

Laurence groaned. "You know how I hate receiving people," he said. "It's nearly as bad as making speeches or telling funny stories at farmers' dinners. All right, I promise."

"And you, Andrew?" said Valentine, turning to her brother.

"Bully. All right, I promise to blow the horn when required. Will that do?" he asked.

"And Sandy and Kate have got to be sociable and introduce people to each other and help arrange the flowers the day before," said Valentine.

"But you know I'm hopeless at introducing people," said Kate. "I shall only upset someone's wine all over someone else's white model dress from Paris; and I never know anyone's names anyway; and you know I can't arrange flowers."

But Valentine hardly heard her sister. She was scribbling names furiously on a sheet of paper on her knee.

"Lucky people to be invited," said Laurence, glancing over her shoulder . "But hadn't we better arrange the date?"

"Hadn't we better see first when the country club can have us," said Valentine.

Laurence told Valentine the name of the club so that she could ring it up at lunch-time. He promised to see Colonel Hayward about using Melcham for the hunter trials, before nightfall. He and I helped feed hounds and watched the Days turn their horses out in the big field at the back of the farmhouse. Then we walked home full of plans for the hunter trials and hunt ball.

FOUR

During the next few days our plans for the hunter trials and hunt ball advanced with encouraging rapidity. Valentine booked the ballroom, the dining-room and a bar for a Friday night at the end of April at the country club Laurence had suggested.

Laurence saw Colonel Hayward, told him our troubles and received permission to use Melcham for our hunter trials. We drafted a schedule; we designed invitation cards; and arranged for a couple of hundred to be printed of each. We discussed bands endlessly, with our parents and with our few friends and acquaintances who attend balls. But none of them were much help. They only said: "For goodness' sake, don't have Bill Still's quartet," or, "For the love of Mike, avoid Dickens' like you would a plague, it's all string and out of tune at that," or, "But my dear, I may go to dances, but I know nothing at all about bands." It was very disheartening; not one had a sensible suggestion to make, and eventually, in despair, Valentine booked a band which advertised in *Horse and Hound*, and a local discotheque.

On Wednesday, having fed hounds and exercised our horses, we all squashed into the Days' landrover and, armed with saws, forks, spades, bill-hooks, hammers, nails, wire and wire cutters, we descended on Melcham to arrange the hunter trial course.

It was a wet day. It had dawned wet, with rain falling from a grey sky. The wind was in the east. The landscape looked uninspiring, cold and bleak. As Kate said, it was maddening to have such weather on the first day of April, when one expected blue skies, sunshine and showers.

Laurence, who had already walked the course suggested by Colonel Hayward, directed Andrew to a gate on the left side of the Allate road. We parked the landrover and then, shouldering the larger of our implements and pocketing the rest, we climbed the gate into a large grass field.

"There's the hill where Colonel Hayward and I thought we could have the judge's wagon," said Laurence, pointing across plough to where another field of grass sloped slowly upwards to a hill topped by a few pines.

"Looks ideal," said Andrew. "Has Colonel Hayward got a wagon? Or have we got to use ours?"

"I didn't ask him, actually," said Laurence. "But he didn't offer one, so I think we'd better use yours."

The wind was blowing straight into our faces. Kate shivered. "It'll be awful if it's like this on the day," she said.

"My hands are like ice," grumbled Harry.

"These spades are a fearful weight," said Valentine. "I'm sure we needn't have brought so many."

"They can't be as heavy as the forks and this awful billhook," said Laurence.

"Oh, I've dropped the nails," cried Kate, throwing the implements she was carrying in a disordered heap and beginning to search frantically in the grass. We stopped and picked up the nails, and Kate's hair, which is naturally wavy, curled in the rain, and mine, which is sandy-coloured and naturally straight, grew lank. Valentine had a handkerchief over her head, which ran until the collar of her shirt was blood red. At last we had picked up all the nails. We sighed with relief and then Kate cried: "I've lost the wire cutters," and because they were Andrew's and the special swan-necked pair which he carried strapped to his saddle on hunting days, we all had to search for them. We grew steadily wetter and our hands had started to ache with cold when Laurence found the cutters under his feet in a clump of grass.

We shouldered our tools again and without a word walked on until we came to a hedge we all remembered, having jumped it many times hunting. We found some rails standing in a corner, and another hedge, with a ditch in front.

Slowly, the course took shape. It was to be circular and in the centre there would be the hill, crowned by the judge's wagon. We were very cold. The land was open and there was no escape from the wind. Valentine, Andrew and Laurence were wearing Barbours, but Kate, Harry and I had shown less sense and were in riding coats. Harry grumbled and slowly the rain seeped through our coats to the clothes beneath. We decided exactly where the hedges were to be flagged, and

Valentine and Laurence hacked at one with a hatchet and billhook, while the rest of us dug the ditch in front. Working warmed us and, though we scratched our hands, tore our clothes and were overcome by backache, we felt more cheerful. We ceased noticing the cold, persistent rain, and we began to talk again and laugh.

When we had finished altering the hedges, except for their final trimming with clippers, which we would do nearer the day, we decided where the start and finish would be. After that, we wandered across heavy plough for what seemed hours, but which was really only minutes; and our legs ached and our backs ached; and our shoulders and arms ached under the weight of the tools we were carrying.

We all wondered whether the hunter trials were really worth such suffering, and everyone thought they were carrying more than anyone else.

At last we came to a lane and Laurence said: "Here's the in and out," and pointed to a hedge into, and a gate out of, the lane. "Of course, we'll have to put down peat moss," he said.

"Another expense," sighed Valentine.

Laurence didn't hear. He was already attacking the hedge with a billhook with terrific ferocity. Kate found some wire and joyfully cut it into small pieces with the cutters.

Andrew crawled through the hedge, which was high and full of brambles, and I followed. He paced across the lane and said: "There'll be room for one stride before you take off again." He looked at the gate, which was wide and solid and roughly four feet in height. "This will be the most difficult jump in the course," he said.

Valentine, Kate and Harry were all helping Laurence, and so Andrew and I wandered across to where some rails, which we had noticed earlier, stood in the corner of a field of wheat. The rails were long and firm and not more than three feet six in height.

"It's going to be difficult to make the course suitable both for children and for the open class," said Andrew. "The children will have to jump into a different part of the lane, I suppose; and that means more peat moss, which is a nuisance. We'll have to take this top rail down and nail it up again between the classes, and somehow we've got to get enough flags."

Andrew sounded depressed. I suddenly realised that he still had no confidence in Laurence's plans and that he was only helping with the hunter trials to please Laurence and myself.

I shivered. The rain was falling in heavy, grey sheets. Although it was only four o'clock on an April day, dusk seemed very near and the grey sky was even greyer than before.

"One thing is, they'll be wide enough for a three," I said, and, at the same moment, my teeth started to chatter.

"It's time we went home," said Andrew. "It's setting in for a wet night." He turned up the collar of his Barbour. In the distance I could see the Chidlington bus splashing along the wet Allate road. "You look like a drowned rat," Andrew said.

We rejoined the others, who had stopped working and were gazing across towards the railway line.

"We're arguing about the trains," Laurence said. "Whether they go to London that way."

"I wouldn't know," said Andrew. "I only go once in five years."

That seemed to end the argument. We shouldered our implements and plodded back to the car. The plough seemed even heavier than before.

On the way home we discussed our entries. Kate thought that Dusty, Daystar and Overture should go together as our three, but Laurence wasn't ready to agree. I don't think he wanted to go with Kate, and he wanted Andrew to be in the team.

"We can't really decide anything until we've practised, anyway," said Andrew. "What about starting tomorrow morning and coming up here again in the afternoon? The practice will have to be early, though, because I've promised Dad I'd slip in to the market at about twelve and see what price the cattle are fetching."

Did that mean the Days were selling their stock already? I wondered, and immediately felt gloomy.

"Let's start at eight," said Kate, who likes to rise at six every morning.

"That's much too early," said Laurence. "Surely half-past nine will do?"

In the end we fixed the practice for ten o'clock, which would allow Andrew at least an hour before he must leave for Hettington market.

The next few days passed all too quickly. The hunter trial practice took hours and Andrew had to leave long before anything was settled. None of the horses jumped alike. Mulligatawny took his fences quietly, slowing up on the approach of each so that he could inspect it before jumping—the Days called it "putting on his spectacles"; Overture jumped with far more scope than the others, which meant that though her partners might be dead level as she took off, when she landed she was always half a length ahead. Daystar liked to jump very fast, much faster than any of the Day's horses, but in spite of this she and Dusty made the best pair. I decided to jump in the pairs, the Chill Valley and Adjacent Hunts class, and the threes, if I were chosen. I hoped that three classes would not prove too many for Daystar. I decided that if the going was heavy I would cancel one of my entries, but which one I could not decide.

After another practice, which lasted for two and a half hours and left us all exhausted and disheartened, it was decided that Andrew, Laurence and I should represent the hunt in the threes class on our own horses; that Andrew should also enter for the open class and the pairs with Valentine; that Kate should enter for the pairs with me, and the class for people under sixteen—she was the only one of us young enough to compete; that Valentine should enter for the Chill Valley and Adjacent Hunts class, as well as the pairs with Andrew; and Laurence, the team, the open, and the Chill Valley and Adjacent Hunts class if the going wasn't too heavy.

Our entry fees came to a great deal of money. Laurence's and mine cost twelve pounds and we had to borrow from Mummy, because we only had ten pounds, eleven pence between us. The Days' came to even more and they had to borrow from Harry's Post Office account to pay them.

"We'll have to be let off buying tickets for the ball," said Kate. "That is if we all really have to go."

"We'll have to win lots at the hunter trials, you mean," said Valentine.

"But we can't," said Andrew. "It's dreadful to win everything at your own hunter trials. One thing is, people can't be spiteful. I mean it's not as though we've jumped one of the fences as they are now. They can't say we've practised, or anything like that."

"Not possibly," said Kate laughing.

"Anyway, we probably won't win anything," said Laurence.

"The schedules should be here by tomorrow," said Valentine.

The advertisement for our ball had already appeared in the local papers; in the same issue of the *Chidlington Mail* as a dreadful photograph of the meet at Little Hall and a description of our hunt in a column headed "Events of the Week." The photograph was of Laurence addressing the children. Laurence had his hands clasped together and looked as though he was praying. Kate and I were in it too, and hounds. Kate was smiling her broadest smile, which shows all her teeth and makes her look like a typical English schoolgirl. I was scowling as usual. Both our horses had their ears back.

The report in "Events of the Week" was only partially true, but was excellent propaganda. It described our pack as compact and sporting. It said that our young, enthusiastic Master had addressed the children in firm, forceful tones, and it reproduced a shortened version of Laurence's lecture. It described Kate and me as "dashing, well-mounted lady whips," and Andrew as "the young serious amateur huntsman." It finished by saying that we had shown great sport during the season, killing several brace of foxes.

At first the Days heralded the report with jubilation, but soon they were saying: "Of course, it *would* come too late,"

"If only we weren't giving up, what a lot of good it might have done us, it might have brought us dozens of new subscribers," Kate said in her dreariest voice.

"It'll still entice people to our hunter trials," said Laurence. "Anyway, how do you know we are giving up?"

By the silence which followed, I knew the Days were still without hope as far as the hunt was concerned.

We had advertised the hunter trials and, long before the schedules were ready, Laurence, who had agreed to be secretary, was receiving letters asking for them.

Valentine had already received a great many inquiries about the ball and had sold several tickets.

With the third day of April, spring returned. The sun shone from a blue sky and everywhere the trees were breaking into bud. Chastity's puppies arrived: three couple, one of which died later. We spent ages choosing names for them. They had to begin with R, because Rattler was their father. Eventually we chose Raiment, Rory, Romeo, Roma, Romper and Rosa. Raiment died two days later and Kate cried.

Little Hall was gradually flooded by letters about the hunter trials. They covered the dining-room table, until Daddy became exasperated. He asked Laurence whether the dining-room had now become his office, and the letters were hastily evacuated to another room where they lay in heaps on every available piece of furniture.

Mummy's smart London friends bought sixteen tickets for the ball and booked a table. Mr. Austin

Smith bought twelve and Colonel Hayward six. Soon Valentine was for ever at the Post Office buying stamps and Laurence for ever typing, until Mummy and I felt we would go mad. All of us were permanently short of time and always in a hurry.

We rose at dawn and retired to bed at midnight. We schooled our horses frantically; and we schooled Lost Horizon, who was a stargazer and who we rode in a standing martingale and a rubber snaffle. She was very nervous of her mouth and very fidgety. Andrew rode her once and said: "Never again," and "No wonder she was a present."

Kate tried her and, afterwards, she said that she liked sensible horses like Dusty and that Lost Horizon was silly and had no brains. Valentine was too busy arranging the ball and attending to her secretarial course to have any time for schooling another horse besides Golden Syrup.

So Lost Horizon became Laurence's and mine to school and we installed her in the paddock at home, because our horses would be staying in until after the trials. We made a practice hunter trial course across the valley, and, though we were often tired and cross, we were happy; happier than we had been for weeks.

Valentine tried frantically to keep down expenses. Already it seemed we must spend a great deal on the ball and also on the hunter trials. She launched a prize fund and Colonel Hayward presented us with a handsome cup for the children's class and Mr. Austin Smith sent us a cheque for ten pounds. Thoughts of money kept her and Laurence awake at night and they talked about expenses endlessly.

Gradually Lost Horizon began to improve. She

learned to extend her neck and no longer carried it in an inside out position. Laurence and I began to ride her over bars on the ground, which we slowly raised until she was jumping a foot high quite calmly. We taught her the turn on the forehand and practised halting until she would halt quietly when we shut our fingers on the reins. When we were riding Overture and Daystar, we spent a great deal of the time without stirrups, so as to improve our own seats, of which we were not proud.

The evenings became lighter. In the garden behind Long Chill Farmhouse there were chicks and ducklings on the lawn in coops and runs. Wasteful's puppies arrived—two couple this time—and once again we had to think of names. Tempest was the father, so their names had to begin with T. Hounds can only have hound names and once again we consulted our list and, after some dispute, chose Tawny, Tapestry, Tyrant and Torchlight as their names. Except for Torchlight, they were large dark puppies and none of them looked like dying. Torchlight had the most white on him and Tawny the least.

We came to the end of the second week in April and the hunter trials seemed dangerously near. The weather was wonderful; the sky seemed always blue and, in the morning the cuckoo would be calling outside my bedroom window. It was a perfect spring. The best spring for years, so everyone was saying.

The day came when Valentine said: "We're sold out. The secretary of the club forbade me to sell more than a hundred and fifty tickets and I've sold a hundred and fifty-one."

Laurence did some quick arithmetic. "Two thousand plus" he said. "It's fantastic."

"The bank must be having a fit," cried Kate, "since usually we're on the verge of an overdraft."

"Of course, the catering's going to cost a lot," said Valentine,

"I must add up my entry money," said Laurence. "I know there are twenty-five entries already in the open class."

"Let's hope for some late entries as well," said Kate.

Major Sunderland, M.F.H., and Mr. Peterson, M.F.H., had agreed to judge. Mr. Peterson had written Valentine a long letter on behalf of both of them. They were coming by car and so had refused our offer to meet them at either Chidlington or Hettington station, much to our relief.

We all read Mr. Peterson's letter in turn and then Andrew said: "What are we going to do about their lunch? They'll have to have a special one, with wine and napkins and flowers on the table."

"And drinks beforehand," said Laurence.

"Another expense," sighed Valentine.

"What's the matter with you, Valentine?" asked Laurence. "It used to be me who was called miserly. Now I seem a positive rake compared with you."

"It's you who've changed," said Valentine. "I suppose it's because you're going up to Oxford and want to practise being extravagant first."

"Practise being extravagant!" exclaimed Laurence. "How much money do you think I'm going to have? I shan't have any to spare."

"We ought to ask some of the officials as well," said Andrew, still talking about the judges' lunch.

"The White Lion Hotel has agreed to be responsible for the refreshments on the field," said Laurence.

"They're erecting a couple of tents, so doubtless they'll supply a special lunch, if I ask them nicely."

"You mean in a tent?" asked Kate.

"Yes, in part of one," replied Laurence.

"That's fine," said Andrew. "They're sure to do it properly. As long as we don't have it in Colonel Hayward's dining-room I don't care where it is."

I knew what Andrew meant. Colonel Hayward is very nice. He's generous, too, and had always taken a great interest in our pack. But if he helps with anything, he's always running it completely before you know where you are, and the function becomes Colonel Hayward's instead of belonging to the hunt.

Already he had appointed himself official starter; he had also offered to judge, an offer which we had tactfully refused. Obviously, he was one of the officials we should have to invite to the special lunch.

"We'll need stewards," Laurence said.

Later, he appointed Patience and Felicity Hayward as stewards; and Bert Saunders agreed to repair any fences which were broken down during the day.

"We still need a secretary on the field and someone at the gate," Andrew said.

We had put up a great many posters advertising our hunter trials. There were two dozen or more scattered around Hettington and Chidlington, in the markets and the saddlery shops, in butchers and grocers, in the station, and in the windows of houses belonging to acquaintances and friends. We had stuck up a good many too, around the countryside, in shops and on telegraph poles and a few on local notice boards, when we discovered who owned them and managed to get permission. Because of these posters, we expected a large "gate," and it was obvious that we should need several really competent people to catch the cars as they came in. We were not charging any entrance money for spectators on foot, but we hoped to sell them programmes at 50 pence each.

Laurence and I racked our brains endlessly to find a secretary and, at last, Mummy grew so tired of the subject that she offered us her services for the day. The secretary disposed of left us with only people for the gate to find. Mr. Mitchell, who helps us with Daystar and Overture sometimes and looks after the garden at Little Hall, came to our rescue. He volunteered to watch the gate and ticket the cars along with his son Herbert and his brother Sid. We were overjoyed; at last everything seemed settled.

But our joy was short-lived. "What about my tent?" Mummy asked. "And have you done anything about the flags?" We searched frantically for a tent. Mummy bought rolls of red and white material and we cut poles out of Badger's Copse and, putting the two together, we made dozens of flags.

We managed to borrow a tent from the Allate Women's Institute. It was rather small and looked fragile and we all prayed that there wouldn't be a wind on the day of our hunter trials.

Once again we thought everything was settled; until Laurence remembered that we had no programme sellers and then the search began again. Although we and the Days had lived in Little Hall and Long Chill Farm for three years, we'd made incredibly few friends. We hadn't needed them until now; occupied with the hunt and our horses, we'd had no time for tea parties, tennis parties and the sort of social functions people of our age attend. Now we found we had no friends of our own age whom we could entrust with the comparatively easy task of selling programmes. "We can't very well ask grown-ups," said Kate, and we all agreed.

Eventually, Valentine contacted girls she had known at school and persuaded them into selling programmes, bribing them with the promise of a special tea afterwards in a special tent. "And that'll be another expense," she sighed when she told us.

When we had a spare moment, Laurence and I contrived to school our horses. Lost Horizon was beginning to go really well on occasions—or so we thought—and we were very pleased with her. We had made our jumps wider rather than higher and she was now jumping bars two feet six high and six feet apart. She was far less nervous, and as she started to lose her winter coat, we could see that she would be a lovely rich bay in colour later on. She was becoming much more sensible. We could now catch her easily, and her head-carriage was improving every day. Daystar and Overture had improved too. They were jumping well with plenty of scope, and with the help of a book on dressage we were beginning to teach them work on two tracks.

The Days thought our schooling effort rather peculiar. Andrew belongs to the single-reined snaffle and running martingale brigade. He likes a horse to be handy across country, and if he jumps well into the bargain he's quite content. He rides mostly with one hand on a loose rein, and sticks his legs rather too far forward. If a horse pulls with him he cuts down the oats and increases the work. Valentine and Kate are much the same; though Valentine lacks the dash of Kate and Andrew's riding. Theirs always makes me think of modern hunting pictures. Andrew and Kate always expect their horses to go with them. They ride at the most awkward fences; down ghastly slopes studded with tree stumps; down precipitous banks on to main roads with surfaces like glass; over and into streams and rivers; through gardens, alleys, camps and even bus garages, and because they never hesitate but throw their hearts over, down or through, their horses go with them. Hunting, they say, is the finest form of education for a horse; though they're the first to admit that an unschooled horse is a menace and a nuisance in the hunting field. The Days prepared their horses for the hunter trials by jumping the course across the valley every two or three days and by long hacks to keep them fit.

As the ball was on the last Friday in April, we didn't have to bother about dresses, and flowers, and transport to it and back until after the hunter trials. I tried to forget it altogether and nearly succeeded. Only sometimes in the middle of the night, or in the early morning, I would remember that it lay ahead, waiting like a mountain to be climbed or a glacier crossed, a forbidding task from which there was no escape.

The day for our last practice for the hunter trials came, and it rained and the wind veered to the north and we all wondered whether the spell of fine weather was breaking up at last.

Kate and I rode round our practice course first as a pair. The horses were very excited, I suppose because it was cold, and the ground was wet and slippy. We seemed to go faster and faster and, when we came to the last fence, Daystar checked and took off right underneath it, and Dusty took off miles in front. We landed with a length between us and, when we reached the winning post, Valentine said: "You didn't keep very well together," and Andrew said: "You looked as though you were winning a point to point," Laurence said: "You won't win anything if you get out of control," and Harry said: "That looked awful." Kate and I knew all this already. Being told what you already know is always irritating, and I wasn't surprised when Kate said: "Well, we didn't do it on purpose. It's the rain; the ground's awful, and the reins just slip through your fingers."

"Do you think we'd better go again?" I asked.

"*A bad workman blames his tools*," chanted Harry, in an irritating voice.

"No, there isn't time," said Laurence. "Besides, you've got to go again in half a sec with Andrew and me."

Valentine and Andrew kept beautifully together but they were rather slow. We timed them and they took three and a half minutes, whereas Kate and I had taken just under three.

Then, after Mulligatawny had regained his breath, we decided to practise as a team. We had received ten entries for this class, two of them representing packs in Leicestershire, and we were particularly anxious to do well and send up the prestige of the Chill Valley Hunt.

Andrew was to ride on the inside, because Mulligatawny is slightly slower than Overture and Daystar. Laurence was riding on the outside and I was squashed between the two of them. Andrew was in charge and set the pace, so that Laurence and I had to keep level with him, which wasn't easy. Kate had been right when she said the reins were slippery. It was raining harder than before, when Andrew, Laurence and I rode round the course together, and Daystar was fighting fit. In vain Andrew cried: "Slower, slower," as we approached every fence; Overture and Daystar increased their pace with one accord, and we landed far ahead in the next field, Overture first, but Daystar close behind. All three of us were quite exhausted by the time we reached the finishing post and Andrew was hoarse from shouting.

"That's hopeless," said Valentine.

"You don't need to tell us," said Andrew.

We stood with slack reins. All too clearly the three of us saw the day after tomorrow, and rode round the course, in our imagination, as we had ridden round the practice course a minute ago.

"It'll be a terrible disgrace," said Andrew.

"Do you think you ought to scratch?" asked Valentine. "No one need know. I'll just delete our entry from the list, and everyone will think we just haven't bothered to enter,"

"And are jolly feeble," said Andrew.

"We can't possibly," said Laurence.

"What about trying again?" I suggested, picking up my reins, which were running with grease. "We may do better a second time."

We rode round the course again, and Andrew shouted even louder than before and, though we stayed together between the fences, we were still miles apart as we jumped.

We came to the end and we all stood together completely disheartened. We were covered with mud; we were wet; and there seemed little left to say. Daystar was tired. She stood with her head drooping. Yet I'm sure, if I had ridden her round the course again, she would have gone just as fast. I didn't love her at that moment.

"We might as well go down," said Andrew as a fresh sheet of rain swept across the valley.

"It'll be lovely if it's like this the day after tomorrow," said Kate sarcastically.

"Some of us had better go to Melcham this afternoon and finish the course," said Andrew. "We won't have much time tomorrow."

I had ceased looking forward to the hunter trials. I saw a wet day and no eager car drivers pressing five pound notes into Mr. Mitchell's, Herbert's and Sid's hands. There'll be just three cars, I thought, ours, the Days and the judges, and instead of making a hundred and fifty pounds we'll lose a hundred. We'll run away in the three classes, I thought, and I shall lose my way in the first class, though, goodness knows, I should know the course by now; and either Kate or I will take a toss in the pairs. Once again, the Chill Valley Foxhounds will be disgraced and will become the laughing stock of the hunting world.

Valentine and Laurence were arguing about money. I wondered why we were so ambitious—we're just conceited, I thought. We should have started by running small hunter trials for the local children, I decided, instead of immense ones with thirty-pound prizes.

"Home, and do cheer up," cried Laurence in exasperated accents.

I realised that we had reached the farm.

"Can't we have another practice tomorrow?" I asked.

The Days were putting their horses away.

"No, apparently Andrew's going to London for his father tomorrow," said Laurence, sounding still more exasperated.

We rode home along the track we love so much in gloomy, hopeless silence.

FIVE

The day before the hunter trials was endless and unforgettable. It rained, and, once again, we were doomed to shiver amid Melcham's open fields. It was raining when we wakened, and the sky was a dreary grey. A breeze stirred the trees. Valentine and Laurence started to quarrel about money from the moment they met. We had borrowed the Days' landrover and, because Andrew was in London, Laurence was driving. He had only recently passed his test and the crosser he became, the faster he drove. Kate and I were nervous wrecks by the time we reached Melcham, and Valentine and Laurence were hardly on speaking terms. To make matters worse, I broke a window, lifting out the flags, and, though Valentine said: "It doesn't matter a bit," and Kate: "For goodness' sake, don't make a mountain out of a molehill," I knew they were cross and already thinking of the most tactful way to explain the accident to their father.

I had wakened determined to be cheerful, but I found it difficult, labouring across the first of the open fields, my back bowed under the weight of flags and my spirits damped by the gloominess of my companions.

We reached the starting post and Laurence unpacked the tent. He refused all offers of help, so Valentine, Kate and I walked round the course sticking up the flags; red on the right of the fences and white on the left, and a few at corners, which competitors were to keep outside.

"What's the matter with your brother today?" Valentine asked. "He seems in no end of a mood."

After a moment's thought, I said: "Worries. Money chiefly and the endless rush; you know how it all gets you down."

Valentine nodded. "He's doing too much, of course," she said.

We had brought Pick, Shovel and Quinky with us. They were rabbiting busily in the hedges.

"We should know the course by the end of the day," Valentine said, as we reached the in and out. "We'll be mad if we go wrong."

"I bet I do, though," said Kate. "I always do the wrong thing if it's humanly possible. I bet when I'm lined up at the start, I shan't remember which coloured flag I leave on my left and which on my right."

"But it's so easy," said Valentine. "Think of the two R's going together—red and right."

"I know it's easy, it nearly always is. That's what makes it so maddening when I forget," Kate answered.

I wondered whether I would lose my way on the course. Several times I had repeated the order of the jumps to myself before falling asleep at night. But that was no guarantee, I thought now, I may still forget. I shall have to keep thinking of the next jump all the way round.

Kate was talking to herself as we walked: "Hedge,

rails, turn left, hedge with ditch in front, rails with ditch on landing, hedge, in and out, gates," she muttered. And then the rain stopped falling, and high in the sky we could see the outlines of the sun.

The tent was lying in a heap when Valentine, Kate and I returned to the starting post. It was very dirty. So was Laurence. His hair had fallen over his forehead like a forelock; his hands, feet, knees and face were covered in mud. He was sitting on the ground, nursing a mallet, in an attitude of complete and utter despair.

"It's no good," he cried, as we approached. "It's hopeless; it's too small. It's hardly more than a children's tent really. It'll never stand up to being a secretary's tent to-morrow."

Valentine looked at the sodden, muddy heap of canvas and guy ropes. Laurence stood up and dusted his knees with his muddy hands which made them muddier.

"In the days of my extreme youth I was once a Girl Guide," Valentine said. She began to shake out the canvas.

Laurence watched her. "It's hopeless," he said again. "It's the wrong kind of tent. I can't see why the Women's Institute, if they must have tents, can't have proper ones."

I was glad Harry wasn't there to say "A bad workman blames his tools." Valentine stuck a couple of tent poles into the ground.

"Someone take hold of the other side," she said, lifting the canvas. After that we all helped. Valentine directed and, before ten minutes had elapsed, the tent was up and securely fastened by guy ropes.

"You should have shrieked for help," Valentine told

Laurence as we set off across the field towards the first of the hedges waiting to be clipped.

It was long past lunch-time when Laurence and I returned home. The course was ready for the first competitor; but we still had our horses to exercise and groom, our tack to clean and our clothes to press, sponge, brush and perhaps even mend. There was hot-pot and roly-poly pudding waiting for us in the simmering oven. We ate quickly, before dashing out to the stable and putting tack on our incredibly dirty horses.

The sky had cleared. Soon there would be sunshine. We took Daystar and Overture out for an hour. They were very quiet and quite different from the day before. After yesterday's disastrous practice, I had decided to cut down Daystar's oats to practically nil for the time being. Now, I nearly changed my mind. It would be dreadful on the morrow if she was sluggish. She might knock the rails, or take off too near her fences to clear the ditches on the landing side. I shouldn't know how to ride her I realised; it would be a terrible experience. But Laurence was against the horses having any oats at all, and finally I decided to give Daystar two small feeds, one after dinner, and one in the morning, half an hour before leaving for Melcham. I recommended Laurence to give Overture the same.

After our ride, I spent hours washing Daystar, first with horse shampoo and then with Showhite. I dried her with my bath towel. Laurence did much the same to Overture, missing out the Showhite and using his own towel. By the time we had finished and bandaged their legs and tails, we were already a quarter of an hour late for tea.

The house was terribly untidy inside. Laurence's papers had overflowed into the passages, where they lay in every corner, on every window-sill and on every available piece of furniture. Recently they had reached the hall and we found Mummy collecting them together before Daddy returned. Of course we helped, and precious minutes passed and were lost, and I wondered whether we could possibly finish our many tasks before another day dawned. We ate tea and afterwards we cleaned out the loose-boxes and settled the horses for the night. When we had finished it was dinner-time and we still had our tack to clean and our clothes to get ready.

We had become steadily more absent-minded throughout the day; after dinner we lost everything—saddle soap, dusters, sponges, our boot bone, our hats, our gloves, they all seemed equally bewitched. We even lost large objects like our breeches and the horses' day rugs, which we had brought indoors to brush. We put our bridles together wrong and Laurence absent-mindedly put boot polish on his saddle in mistake for saddle soap. The kitchen, where we were working, soon looked like nowhere on earth, least of all a kitchen.

It was worse still when ten o'clock came and Mummy arrived on the scene, wishing to fill hot-water bottles and put cups and saucers ready for the early morning tea. She found the crockery on the dresser covered with a mixture of boot polish, saddle soap, metal polish and mud, and, as you can imagine, she was far from pleased. She washed piles of cups, plates and saucers, but she wouldn't let us help. We felt awful and horribly disheartened, struggling with our tack, which was unusually stiff and refused to grow supple in spite of a combination of neatsfoot oil, saddle soap and elbow grease.

"Never again," Laurence kept muttering to himself, "never again," and when Mummy asked him what he meant, he said: "Hunter trials. Never again shall I run them."

I had ceased to care about the morrow. I only wanted to finish cleaning my tack and clothes and go to bed.

Outside, the moon had risen and the yard and garden were silver and full of shadows. If I hadn't been disheartened, I should have been overjoyed to behold such promise of fine weather to come.

At last our tack and clothes were ready for the morrow, and we collapsed against the Aga stove and drank tea and ate thick slices of slab cake. We were too sleepy for conversation and when the church clock at Allate struck eleven across the silent fields we climbed the stairs to bed.

Saturday dawned fine. It was dark when Laurence and I rose at five o'clock, but later the sky was lit by a fiery red glow, which gradually spread from east to west and from north to south. Laurence and I both wakened with hopeful hearts. I seemed hardly to have slept at all. Minutes might have passed instead of hours, between cleaning tack in the kitchen and hearing the alarm ringing in the passage outside my door. It was easy to jump out of bed, switch off the alarm and waken Laurence. My clothes were waiting for me. The horses were clean. Just as yesterday was set for failure, today seemed set for success. Laurence and I whistled as we mucked out the boxes in semi-darkness and, as light came, groomed our horses. We carried a schedule of the day's work in our heads, and by half-past six, when we ate breakfast and called our parents, we were already half an hour ahead of it.

"I wonder how the Days are getting on. I bet they're in a rush," said Laurence smugly.

I quoted: "*Pride comes before a fall.*" By seven-thirty, our horses were plaited, saddled and munching feeds. We dressed carefully in hunting kit, put day rugs, grooming tools and a sack of feed in the car and then bridling our horses, we mounted and rode away across the valley.

The morning was perfect. The whole countryside seemed to sparkle beneath the sun. Our horses felt fresh, but not too fresh, and looking at each other, we agreed that we were both perfectly attired for hunter trials. The Days were waiting for us. They were immaculate too, in their hunting clothes, their horses plaited, their tack gleaming in the sunlight.

We rode away towards Allate. We refused to think of the hunter trials. We discussed the weather, and our horses' manners, and our struggles of the evening before.

For ages I was sure I had left something behind. I checked all the things I should have with me and then I realised suddenly what it was I missed—hounds. Hounds behind me, on each side of me, travelling along the road in the sunlight, their sterns high, their eyes happy and alert. Never before had Laurence and I and the Days ridden together through Allate in hunting kit without our pack around us. It was a strange feeling. I looked at Andrew, slightly odd in black instead of scarlet, and he grinned and said: "The road seems empty without them, doesn't it?" and I realised how much we and the Days had come together since we first started the Chill Valley Hunt.

The open fields of Melcham looked large and beautiful in the sunlight. We could see Mummy, who had raced us in the car, installing herself in the secretary's tent.

"It's half-past nine, and they're due to start at ten," said Laurence, as we reached the entrance gate and Mr. Mitchell waved us through.

"The judges should be here any moment now," said Valentine.

"And one of us will have to walk round the course with them," said Andrew.

"Laurence. He's secretary," said Valentine.

Crates of beer were being carried into the larger of the refreshment tents. The judge's wagon, which Andrew had towed by tractor from Long Chill Farm the evening before, looked lost standing alone amid the pines on the hilltop. Bert Saunders had arrived and was walking round the course with a hammer in his hand. A few men stood outside the tents with dish cloths and buckets in their hands.

I couldn't believe that in half an hour the field would be full of horses and everything would be ready.

We walked across to the secretary's tent and the Days collected their numbers from Mummy; Laurence and I had removed ours from the pile the day before.

A horse-box turned in at the entrance and I saw another one behind. Colonel Hayward was coming towards us carrying a shooting stick and wearing a checked cloth cap.

"That's probably the judges," said Kate, pointing along the Allate road to where a long, low black car was sandwiched between a horse-box and a cattle truck. My tummy was beginning to feel funny. I had never competed in hunter trials before.

Felicity and Patience were receiving their orders for the day from Colonel Hayward and Laurence, but mostly from Colonel Hayward.

I could see Mr. Watson approaching us across country, a liver and white spaniel at his heels. Smart competitors, wearing camel-hair coats over hunting kit, were watching a groom lead their horses out of the first of the horse-boxes.

"Here, hold Overture," said Laurence, handing me his reins.

I saw that the judges were approaching us in the long, low, black car Kate had noticed on the road.

There was a faint breeze blowing, otherwise the land seemed still. The cattle had been moved to yards nearer home. Somewhere in a tree a pigeon was crying, "My toe bleeds, Betty."

Laurence shook the judges by the hand and Colonel Hayward hovered until he was introduced. Then the four of them walked away to look at the course. I looked at my watch and saw that it was twenty to ten. Mr. Austin Smith had arrived and was leading his seventeen-hand grey hunter out of the trailer behind his car. The Honourable David Peterborough was collecting his number from the secretary's tent; his boots and spurs gleamed and sparkled in the sunlight. He had substituted a black coat for his usual scarlet one with swallow tails and the buttons of the East Nightley Hunt.

Laurence had told me that I was to go first in the Chill Valley and Adjacent Hunts' Class.

"Then the other competitors will know the way," he had said, and I, being disheartened at the time, had said nothing. Now I regretted my silence. I wanted to watch other competitors riding first; to see how fast they took their fences, whether they went the same steady pace all the way round or finished with a flourish at the end.

The judges and Colonel Hayward and Laurence had reached the in and out.

There were hoofs on the road and five riders in rat-catcher on big blood horses turned in through the entrance. The sun was screened by clouds. It was eight minutes to ten.

Andrew called: "Will all competitors for Class One get ready, please."

Colonel Hayward returned to the starting post. Laurence was escorting the judges to their wagon. I gave Overture's reins to Harry, who had appeared with Mr. and Mrs. Day. I cantered Daystar in a circle and my stirrups felt different lengths and my hat as though it might fall off.

I altered my stirrups, but they only felt worse, so I altered them back again. I stuck my handkerchief inside the lining of my hat, and pulled up my girths. Colonel Hayward signalled, and taking the megaphone from Andrew announced me as the first competitor. I rode towards him and noticed that Mr. Watson had joined the judges on the wagon.

"Good luck," said Kate.

Laurence passed me as I stood waiting for the signal to start. "Mr. Watson's time-keeping for them," he said. "Apparently we should have provided someone. Good luck."

Colonel Hayward was holding a white handkerchief. "I shall say 'are you ready?' and then 'go,' and drop my hand," he said.

Daystar started to dance. Suddenly I felt optimistic. I'm going to show everyone what the Chill Valley Hunt can do, I thought, and saw Colonel Hayward drop his arm and heard him say "Go."

Beneath Daystar's hoofs the ground felt light and dry. We were over the first hedge before I had time to think. The breeze was in my face. My hat felt firm and my stirrups no longer different lengths. Daystar was keen. Her long easy stride carried her well over the grass. We reached the rails and she took off a long way in front and landed far out into the plough. I was enjoying myself. I had forgotten about our reputation and that there were prizes to be won. I was just crossing a flagged and difficult piece of country with Daystar and it felt wonderful. I remembered to turn left and we took the hedge with the ditch in front rather fast, but we were over with inches to spare. I saw the in and out ahead. I sat down in the saddle and changed Daystar's gallop into a canter. We jumped the hedge into the lane; another stride and we were over the gate and galloping again, towards the finish and the last jump. Daystar didn't feel at all tired; she was galloping well into her bridle and, as we reached the final gates, I pushed her on a little and we cleared them with ease. I let her go her own pace after that and we passed the finishing post at a flat-out gallop. I heard a faint clapping and saw that there was a line of cars on my left with spectators on top and inside.

I dismounted and found that my legs were weak. I patted Daystar and told her that she was the best pony in the world, and loosened her girths. Then I walked across the field to where the Days and Laurence were standing together in a little group.

"Jolly good," they shouted.

I suddenly felt very contented. Even if our hunter trials failed to raise hundreds of pounds, I felt that the work of the last few weeks had not been in vain. Daystar was better schooled; a nicer ride and a more accomplished jumper. I was riding better than I had ever ridden before; and, perhaps most important of all, I had experienced for the first time that wonderful feeling of being completely one with my horse.

"You made jolly good time," said Laurence.

"She jumped beautifully," said Kate.

"I'm next," said Valentine.

Daddy came across from the car in which he had been sitting. "That was a good effort, wasn't it?" he asked, patting Daystar. "It looked pretty polished."

"It wasn't me, it was Daystar," I said. "She was wonderful."

Dozens of people had arrived during the last few minutes and Valentine's school friends were energetically selling programmes. I counted twenty-seven cars parked on the edge of the course, and a coach. There were sporting, horsy-looking people to be seen carrying shooting-sticks and walking-sticks and with binoculars slung across their shoulders. Looking at them Kate said: "East Nightley people, I expect."

David Peterborough was mounting a lively, dark brown hunter which looked as though it was in *the book*. Daddy had gone to the secretary's tent to see whether Mummy needed any help.

"You might win something, you know," said Kate. "It really was a jolly good round."

Everywhere people were discussing the course. "A little short, but nice and clean," was the comment of a tall woman on a heavyweight hunter.

"I don't like the in and out," said a girl on a grey.

"Take it slowly and you'll be all right," advised a youngish man on a bay cob.

I watched Mr. Austin Smith jumping rather slowly on his big grey and I was glad that I had already ridden. There was no need for me to worry any more now until after lunch when I must represent the hunt in the threes and jump in the pairs with Kate.

Mr. Austin Smith jumped the gates and came past the finishing post at a steady, hand gallop. Not far behind him was the next competitor, Mrs. Simmons on her chestnut whose name I always forget. Valentine was waiting at the start, looking calm and detached. Golden Syrup was standing beautifully and gazing into the distance. The next moment they had started. They took the first hedge in fine style; gradually they grew smaller and smaller, and then larger and larger when they had turned for home.

Golden Syrup was jumping well but, as she came to the final gates, she hesitated and then rushed them, knocking the top with her forelegs.

"She's out of it," said Kate, in disappointed accents. "What a shame!"

"I shouldn't be too sure," I said, watching the next competitor refuse three times at the first jump.

There were dozens of entries for Class One; eleven o'clock came and they were still going round. There was a short, sharp burst of rain and, as it finished, I suddenly saw that Laurence had reached the in and out. I was furious with myself for missing so much of his round. Overture took the hedge rather too fast and, landing far out into the lane, she had no room for a stride, and though with an effort she cleared the gate, she jumped awkwardly.

"That's another of those Chill Valley Hunt youngsters," said a man in a cloth cap. "I must say, they do jump!"

I didn't hear his companion's reply.

"He's the last," said Kate, suddenly beside me. "I should think you and David Peterborough have done the best rounds."

Laurence passed the finishing post. He dismounted and came across to us smiling. "Pity about the in and out," he said, "But didn't she jump beautifully? It felt like flying." He patted Overture and gave her a piece of carrot.

"You must be somewhere, Sandy," he said.

"You may be," said Kate.

"Oh, no, I'm nowhere," said Laurence. "I'm sure there's been dozens of rounds better than mine."

The judges were conferring. Colonel Hayward collected the children for the next class. Felicity was waiting by the wagon on the hill for the results. The sun was shining and a rainbow of many colours stretched across the blue sky.

"You'd better mount," Andrew told me, "and pull up your girths."

I was glad that Mr. Watson was on the wagon. Otherwise he would have certainly chosen this moment for conversation. He would have asked me how much

Daystar cost, where my boots had come from, whether I often quarrelled with Laurence, whether I could cook—dozen of questions which he had asked me dozens of times before.

I couldn't believe it when Colonel Hayward announced: "First, Miss Sandy Darlington of the Chill Valley Hunt on Daystar; second, Mr. Peterborough on Sportsman; third, Mr. Laurence Darlington of the Chill Valley Hunt on Overture"—I didn't catch the name of the person who was fourth, but it was no one any of us knew.

Laurence pulled up his girths and mounted hurriedly. Andrew said: "Jolly good." Kate said: "What an advertisement!" I wished Colonel Hayward hadn't put so much emphasis on the Chill Valley Hunt in his announcement. It smacked too much of propaganda for my liking.

"After you," said David Peterborough. We cantered across sunlit grass to the judges' wagon. Daystar was pleased to be leading; she cantered beautifully, with her head high, her jaw relaxed and her tail streaming out behind.

The familiar local Press reporter was lurking behind the wagon. He came forward as we took our rosettes, and I remembered to shut my mouth. I tried to smile, and Daystar pricked her ears.

Major Sunderland said: "The first two of you were very near," and smiled at me and David Peterborough. "It was a matter of twelve seconds between you. Your performances were both faultless."

I patted Daystar. I couldn't think of anything to say.

Mr. Peterson said: "The Chill Valley Hunt seem to

be distinguishing themselves." and he patted Daystar and said: "Rattling good pony."

We all said "Thank you," and David Peterborough and Laurence replaced their hats, which they had removed before receiving their rosettes. I led the way back to the starting post, and the cars and the spectators, and there was a burst of clapping as we approached and someone cried: "Well done, the Chill Valley Hunt," and I wished whoever it was would keep their mouth shut, because I was beginning to wonder whether it was "done" to win first and third prize in the first class at your own hunter trials.

The children's class took till one o'clock. There were twenty-seven entries and fifteen clear rounds. The sun continued to shine from a cloudless blue sky and we were all too hot in our hunting kit. Kate's round was one of the faultless ones. She had jumped Dusty fast, using her legs in front of every fence, and Dusty had jumped beautifully with plenty of scope. Waiting for the results was agony. I wanted Kate to win something, more than I could say. I wanted all of us to have a rosette on our horse's bridle when we left Melcham for home when the hunter trials were over.

We knew that Kate's round had been among the best half dozen. But no one of us was prepared for Colonel Hayward's announcement: "First in Class Two, Miss Kate Day of the Chill Valley Hunt on Dusty." Neither were our fellow competitors, judging by the tone of their conversation. I heard the word "favouritism" and then, quite clearly: "Of course, *they've* practised over it. Dash it all, it's right in their country."

I felt hot with rage, I swung round and saw the girl

on a black blood pony, and couple of women with their hair encased in nets, riding nondescript bay horses. I had no idea which of them had made the remarks and they fell silent under my accusing gaze. I was determined not to let Laurence and the Days know what I had heard, so I held my tongue while inside I was seething with anger at such an unjust accusation.

Kate returned carrying a red rosette. "Isn't it wonderful? We'll match now for the pairs," she said, tying it to Dusty's bridle.

Laurence had been seeing whether everything was ready for the judges' lunch. "Chicken and lobster salad; gâteau, fruit and ice-cream, or cheese," he said. "All washed down by Sauterne."

"Sounds lovely," said Valentine.

"Don't you wish you were invited?" asked Laurence, before walking on to meet the judges and take them in to lunch.

"We'd better water and tie up the horses," said Valentine.

The whips had not been invited to the judges' lunch, and Valentine had declined an invitation on the plea of saving money. So, only Andrew and Laurence were to attend from the Chill Valley Hunt. Their guests would be Mummy, Colonel Hayward, Mr. Watson and, of course, the judges.

Valentine, Kate and I watered, rugged and fed the horses. We left them tied to one of Colonel Hayward's magnificent post and rail fences, and fetched sandwiches and coffee in thermos flasks from the landrover, where Daddy and Mr. and Mrs. Day were having lunch together.

All around us were people eating sumptuous lunches out of superb picnic baskets—chicken, salmon sandwiches, boiled eggs, biscuits and butter. One party had bottles of champagne.

We sat down near the horses and Kate said: "This is much more fun than having a smart lunch with the judges and having to behave ourselves."

Valentine said: "I quite agree. Here we can watch our fellow competitors and it doesn't matter if you upset the salt of if Sandy has a coughing fit, or if I can't think of anything to say."

I wasn't sure whether I agreed with my companions. I should have enjoyed discussing hounds and hunting with Major Sunderland and Mr. Peterson, and I wanted to know exactly how hunter trials are judged.

Harry joined us, dragging Pick and Shovel. "Oh, Harry, what would Andrew say?" Valentine exclaimed. "Can't you let them off for a bit?"

Andrew hates to see the terriers on leads. He says it makes them look like lap dogs. Harry had a piece of rope round each of their necks.

"Surely couples would be better," Kate said. Harry ignored his sisters' remarks.

"I've counted forty-five cars altogether," he said. "Does that mean we've taken two hundred twenty-five pounds?"

"It depends whether you've counted ours and the Darlingtons and the judges in with the forty-five," said Valentine.

"Of course I haven't," answered Harry. "Nor have I counted the ones by the horse-boxes with trailers, nor Colonel Hayward's."

"That's fine," said Valentine. "They'll just about cover all the prize money."

"And there'll probably be lots coming in after lunch," said Kate. "The people who don't get off work till twelve on Saturdays will arrive."

"I hope Susie, Celia and Joan have sold plenty of programmes," said Valentine, alluding to her school friends.

"We mustn't forget their special tea," I said.

"I'm afraid they're going to think it rather a swindle," said Valentine. "They're expecting a sit down tea with ice-cream and meringues and they're going to get a stand up one with the same food as anyone can buy."

"But it'll be for nothing," said Kate. "And they'll be able to eat as much as they like."

"Which should be some consolation," I said.

We were silent for a moment. Then Kate said: "I bet Mr. Watson's talking."

"And Colonel Hayward," added Valentine.

"Actually, I think Mr. Watson's jolly decent stepping into the breach like that and doing the timing," said Kate. "It might have been awkward if he hadn't been there."

"Hear, hear," said Valentine.

"Dear old Watty," exclaimed Harry. "You know, we're winning everything—I mean the hunt is."

"We're not," said Valentine. "We've only won two classes."

"And a third prize," said Harry. "Anyway, there's only been two classes so far. I think we're doing jolly well."

I was beginning to feel sleepy. The sun was hot on my back. I hoped I wouldn't lose control of Daystar in the pairs class, and disgrace the hunt in the threes.

Valentine looked at her watch and said: "Twenty to two. We'd better get cracking. We've got Overture and Mulligatawny to get ready as well as our own horses."

The elegant picnic baskets were being transported back to obscurity in boots and back seats. A few people were already mounted. Next was the open class and the competitors for it, with few exceptions, looked polished horsemen. Most of the horses appeared fit and full of oats, but wise as well, as though hunter trials were an everyday affair.

There's no hope of us winning the Open Class, I thought, and I didn't know whether to be pleased or not.

As we mounted our own horses and prepared to lead Overture and Mulligatawny down to the start, Andrew, Laurence and their guests came out of the refreshment tent. They were talking and laughing.

"Obviously lunch was a success," said Kate.

SIX

"Lunch went off beautifully," said Laurence, laughing and taking Overture from me. "They said it was the best judges' lunch they'd ever eaten."

"Who? Major Sunderland or Mr. Peterson?" asked Valentine.

"How did the others enjoy themselves?" asked Kate.

"Like anything," replied Andrew. "Of course, Major Sunderland wanted to know all about hounds, particularly about Conscript, Ludlow and Spendthrift. He was amazed when he heard they were all hunting and hadn't killed a cur-dog yet." (Killing dogs was one of their vices before we had them, and one of the reasons why they were given to us.)

"Apparently Spendthrift never hunted at all when they had him," said Laurence.

"Of course, Colonel Hayward talked rather a lot," said Andrew. "Mr. Watson was unusually silent. I don't know why."

"Yes, he seemed a bit subdued," said Laurence. "I expect he was exhausted after timekeeping all morning."

"It must be pretty strenuous work, really," said Andrew.

"I don't know about strenuous," said Laurence. "But it certainly needs powers of concentration, which are probably rather lacking in Mr. Watson."

Andrew and Laurence rode down to the start. There were thirty-two entries in the Open Class. Andrew was going third and Laurence twentieth. The first competitor had started. Several more cars had arrived during the lunch interval. The refreshment tents were doing a brisk trade.

"I wish we could go to hunter trials every Saturday all through the summer," said Kate. "Wouldn't it be fun?"

David Peterborough was riding a different horse; a large, beautifully-proportioned chestnut, with a coat which shone in the sunlight, and two gleaming white socks behind.

"Doesn't he look immaculate?" said Kate, glancing at David Peterborough with a critical eye. "Like an advertisement."

"Or a picture," I said. "Someone must have groomed his horse for hours and hours, for months and months."

"I'd rather look sporting," said Kate.

Andrew's turn had come. Mulligatawny stood sensibly at the start, his Roman nose looking more Roman than ever.

"That's their huntsman," someone said.

"Well, if they win this time, I'm going home," their companion replied.

I looked round and saw the two women again, with their hair in nets, sitting astride their bay horses. I stared at them, hoping to stare them out of countenance. I felt hot inside and very angry. Their remarks were particularly infuriating; it wasn't as though we'd ever thought about riding the course before the hunter trials, or that we had expected to win the first two classes.

Their conversation had distracted my attention from the course. Now I saw that Andrew had reached the rails before the in and out. Mulligatawny jumped them, calmly, sensibly, without rushing, but without putting his spectacles on either. I thought: I don't care what those horrid women say; we didn't practise over the course and that's all that matters. Mulligatawny timed the in and out perfectly.

"What did I say?" asked one of the women. "No horse would jump like that without knowing what was coming."

"What nonsense!" cried Kate, with fury in her voice, swinging round in her saddle and facing the women. "What absolute rot. We've never practised over the course."

I hadn't realised that Kate too, had overheard the conversation.

"In fact, we could easily take you up for slander," I said, remembering a past conversation in the dining-room at home. But I spoke only to their backs. They were riding away towards the start. They even might not have heard our remarks.

"Cowards," said Kate loudly. "Horrid, spiteful cowards."

"Ssh," I said.

"I don't care if everyone hears," said Kate defiantly, "and I jolly well hope *they* do."

Andrew and Mulligatawny were passing the winning post. I don't care, I thought, I don't care what anyone says. But all the same I did care. The woman's remarks had spoilt the flavour of our triumphs. It no longer mattered to me whether we won the pairs or not, and I wasn't even sure that I wanted us to win the class for the best three representing any one hunt.

Kate and I rode forward and congratulated Andrew on his round. Mulligatawny was grazing. Andrew stood with the reins looped over his arm watching the next competitor.

"It was clear, wasn't it?" he asked.

Kate and I had to admit that we hadn't seen his entire round. Neither of us mentioned the conversation we had overheard, nor our swift, but ineffective counter-attack.

Fortunately, Laurence had watched Andrew with more concentration. Now he rode forward saying: "Jolly good. It was clear all the way."

I suddenly knew that Andrew was to win the Open Class. It was to be one of those days when success follows success; when one rides better and better every hour. I suspected one of our pairs would win the next class and that our three would be a credit to the Chill Valley Hunt. And our fellow competitors will become angrier and angrier, I thought, and more certain each moment that we have bribed the judges and practised over the course dozens of time before.

The sun was gliding behind clouds, which looked like soft mountains of snow in the blue sky.

Another competitor started. It would be hours before the pairs could begin. Valentine was talking to her parents. Kate and I tied our horses to the rails again. We wandered over to one of the tents and bought sickly cream cakes and soft, flaky jam puffs. Kate was very silent. The man behind the cakes and urns said: "Had a good day,?" And we had to admit that we had. He looked at us rather oddly. I expect he thought we looked pretty miserable for people who had been winning first prizes. We ate our cakes and walked out again. Once more the sun was shining. Laurence was standing by the starting post and we knew it must be his turn soon.

We saw Susie, Celia and Joan. They cried: "Hiya, you two. When are we going to have the tea you promised?" I felt embarrassed. I felt that we were treating them rather badly.

Kate said: "We told you, you wouldn't have it till the end." She sounded quite cross.

"But everything will be finished by then," said Susie, pouting.

I had a sudden brain wave. "Have it now," I said, "I'll fix the manager."

I approached the man behind the tea bar. I said: "Can you let these people behind me have as much as they like to eat, please, and chalk it up to the Chill Valley Hunt?"

He looked at me suspiciously. "I'd better speak to the boss," he said. He returned with a man in a suit, who was very ready to oblige. We left Susie, Joan and Celia with plates of meringues and ice-cream in front of them, and wandered out into the sunlight again.

Laurence was waiting for the signal to start. The two disagreeable women were just behind him.

"It'll be fun to see how they do," said Kate. "We mustn't miss them."

Laurence took the first hedge at a steady hand gallop, but I could see that Overture wanted to rush. Soon she was fighting him and once she threw her head up and he nearly lost control. She increased her pace until she was jumping very fast indeed and though he did a clear, spectacular round, probably in record time, I knew he must have lost marks for his lack of control.

Kate and I walked across and met Laurence as he finished.

"Gosh, she did want to go!" he exclaimed, dismounting. "I hope she's calmer in the threes, otherwise we're done for."

I stopped myself from saying: "Would it matter if we were?" And Kate said: "I should think you made record time."

"She looked simply lovely," said Valentine, suddenly beside us. "And she jumped with tons of scope."

"Next year she'll be simply wonderful," said Laurence. "She just needs a few more months' schooling and then she'll be a three-day event horse. I might be able to ride at Badminton. Just think of it!"

"You'll have to learn dressage first," said Andrew.

"Sandy, we've forgotten the women!" cried Kate, her voice suddenly horrified.

"What is she talking about?" asked Laurence.

I looked across the course and saw that one of them was riding towards the final gates. Her horse's gallop became a canter as she drew near; she sat very still in the saddle with a firm feel on the reins.

"Legs," said Kate. "Legs."

"What a horse!" said Valentine, as the bay put down

his head and charged the gate, smashing a middle bar.

"I shouldn't like to hunt hounds on him," said Andrew.

I caught Kate's eye and knew that she too was trying not to feel pleased.

Bert Saunders appeared as though by magic and repaired the gate. Kate and I forgot to watch the other woman on her bay horse, because Daddy came across, then and talked to us.

"Yours is the fastest time to date," he told Laurence. "I've been timing each one."

We watched a few more competitors and then, once again, we saw Felicity waiting by the wagon for the results.

"Another time we'll install field telephones," said Laurence. "This way of hearing the results is much too slow. And Major Sunderland says we really should have someone at the second hedge, the one with the ditch in front. Apparently they can't see it clearly from the wagon."

"We'll have to write all criticisms down in a book," I said. "We'll never remember them otherwise."

"She's nearly back," cried Kate, her eyes glued to Felicity. "Quick, Andrew, mount. I'm sure you've won something."

"I doubt it," he said, pulling up his girths. "I was too slow. Laurence's was a much better round."

"Nonsense," said Laurence. "I was out of control half the time and you know how judges hate that."

"You may not have been as fast as Laurence, but you were far from slow," Kate told her brother.

Somehow I knew deep down inside me that Andrew had won. Even so, I started with surprise when Colonel

Hayward announced: "First, Mr. Andrew Day, Huntsman to the Chill Valley Foxhounds, riding his own horse, Mulligatawny." The rest of the results were drowned by cheering. Mr. Day and a party of friends were throwing their hats in the air, slapping each other on the back and shouting: "Well done, boy. Well done. Well done, the Chill Valley Hunt."

I looked round hoping to see the faces of the two women on their bay horses, but they were nowhere to be seen. Andrew had mounted. I remembered to congratulate him. He answered: "It's nothing, just luck," and I said: "Nonsense, you've beaten some of the best hunter trial horses in England," and I thought how wonderful it was, and how small Mulligatawny looked as Andrew rode him between his fellow competitors, who were mostly riding large, blood horses built for the shires. Then I saw that Laurence, too, was riding towards the judges' wagon.

"He's reserve," said Kate, in answer to my perplexed face. "Everyone was making such a row none of us heard the whole of the results."

I was very pleased. We'll hang our rosettes in the saddle-room, such as it is, I thought (our saddle-room is part of the garage) and in my imagination I saw them hanging on the wall.

Andrew and Laurence returned and we congratulated them again. After that Kate and I started practising for the pairs. Daystar felt very fresh—fresher than she had been in the morning. Dusty was unusually quiet. We found it difficult to keep together. All around us people were talking about Andrew's win. The local inhabitants were overjoyed. "'E deserves it, every bit of it," someone said. "Great one to hounds, always has been," commented a man wearing a Homburg hat and gaiters. "I've always liked the Days," a woman said. "They're not so stuck up as most children nowadays."

I wondered whether Andrew would like to hear himself being called a child.

"He's got a nice face," another woman said. "Good lot them Days," a huge farmer with a buff waistcoat said. But not all the comments were complimentary; far from it.

"I can't see why they put him first," said a stocky woman on a heavyweight. "He looked desperately slow."

"It's a common sort of a horse, too," said a slim girl with fair wavy hair and lots of lipstick.

"He's another of those Chill Valley Hunt children who run their own pack of hounds," said a man on a chestnut, in disparaging accents.

We picked up tail-ends of conversation as we rode around: "Gave the judges lunch." "Of course, they live quite near." "But, my dear, it's obvious. They bought half their pack from the Waynesborough Hunt, doesn't that explain everything?" Gradually my feeling of anger subsided and a feeling of misery set in.

"What's the good of complaining?" someone demanded.

"I tried," a man butted in. "The woman in the secretary's tent doesn't know a thing, or pretends she doesn't."

I turned round to say something. But Kate said: "They're not worth bothering about. Treat them with contempt," and I let the words die in my throat. Silently, I vowed never to complain about anything at any hunter trials, however unjustly they might be judged.

"Aren't people beastly?" said Kate. "At this moment I hate the whole world. I jolly well hope you win the threes, that'll teach them."

"The pairs are first," I said, thinking how beautiful the landscape looked in the sunlight.

I can hardly bear to describe Kate's and my efforts in the pairs class. The instant we turned towards the starting post Daystar became excited. She jigged and jogged and barged her quarters into Dusty, and, when Colonel Hayward dropped his handkerchief she started like a bullet from a gun.

"Steady," shrieked Kate. "Steady!"

I braced my back and tried to slow the pace, but without avail. Daystar's head was down and she was determined to gallop her fastest. I felt like John Gilpin as we took the first fence and landed far ahead of Kate on the other side. The sun was hot in my face. My hat had slipped.

"Not so fast," shrieked Kate. "I can't keep up."

Daystar knew the course. She seemed determined to make record time. I sat down very hard in the saddle, and raised my hands, and used my legs, my back, and my seat, as I had read you should in one of our books on riding.

"Slower, slower," shrieked Kate, urging Dusty faster and faster.

"I'm trying to go slower," I yelled back. "Can't you gallop faster? Time counts," I added, though I knew that I was going far too fast and that I must be losing hundred of marks for lack of control.

We passed the finishing post with a length between us. Daystar had jumped the last gates far too fast. I looked back and saw them lying in a battered heap on the ground. Once past the finishing post, Daystar's gallop became a canter. I felt limp and horribly disappointed. Without realising it, subconsciously since my victory in the morning I had expected to win something in the pairs.

I dismounted and Kate caught up and said: "That was a disgraceful display. However, doubtless it will please our critics."

"I'm terribly sorry," I said. "I really couldn't go any slower."

"Well, I couldn't go any faster, so really we're quits," said Kate.

Dusty and Daystar looked tired. They were caked with mud and sweat. We loosened their girths. I shall spoil the next class for Andrew and Laurence, I thought, seeing myself streaming away in front of them, while our critics smiled sourly and passed fresh comments. Another pair were riding the course.

"They're better than us," said Kate watching them jump the in and out clear. Valentine and Andrew were next. They stayed well together. Their horses' strides seemed to match as they covered the ground. They made a clear round and Kate cried: "Hurray, I should think they'll be somewhere." We congratulated them as they came past the finishing post.

Andrew shouted: "It felt awful. Were we really together at all?" and Valentine said: "I knocked something somewhere. I heard the sound of splintering wood."

Laurence came across to us and said: "It looks as though the threes class is going to be a bit of a fiasco as far as we're concerned."

"You mean it'll be a race?" said Andrew.

Laurence nodded.

I felt gloomy. "Let's see if there are any ice-creams left," I suggested to Kate. "It's four o'clock and I'm really hungry."

"Shouldn't the judges be sent across some tea?" Laurence asked.

"Yes, definitely," Valentine said.

Kate and I ate ice-creams. "The stewards can take across the judges' tea," said Kate. "It'll look awful if we do. We'll be bribing the judges again."

Mr. Smythe was buying cups of tea and a plate of cakes in the refreshment tent. We had given him a free car park ticket, because he's always arranging draws for us and generally helping the hunt, though in the old days when we first started he was anything but friendly. He shook us both by the hand now and said: "I'm coming to your ball and so's Mrs. Smythe. It'll be the first time we've been to a dance for nearly twenty years."

Kate said: "Oh, I *am* glad," and sounded as though she meant it. I said: "That's wonderful," and Mr. Smythe told us that next season he would give us a lawn meet in February. Neither Kate nor I dared to suggest that our pack might not be in existence then, and I think Mr. Smythe wondered why we received his offer with so little enthusiasm. Lots more people greeted us and congratulated us on our successes, and the success of the hunter trials. Everyone living within a radius of twenty miles of Long Chill Farm seemed to know Kate. Presently, we learned that Andrew and Valentine had won third prize in the pair class, and we left the tea tent to congratulate them. By now, horse-boxes had begun to leave. Only the people competing in the next class remained with their horses. Evening was in the air, and the day had grown cold. Mummy was putting papers together in the secretary's tent.

Kate said: "Good luck," as Andrew, Laurence and I left her for a practice canter together as a three. I still didn't care very much whether we won or not. Daystar seemed quieter and she and Overture looked pleased to be together again. Our turn came second. Before us the team from Leicestershire competed and they made a brilliant round.

"No hope for us, I'm afraid," said Laurence, as they swept past the winning post still beautifully together. The next moment we had started and Andrew was crying: "Keep together; slower, slower. Now!" We increased our pace and were over the first fence well together. Daystar felt calm; she wasn't trying to rush at all. "Steady," yelled Andrew, "keep well together. Now." We were over another jump and still in perfect formation. The first feeling of tension was over. I relaxed, and now nothing seemed to put us wrong; we took off together and landed together, shoulder level with shoulder, knee to knee. I wanted to cry: "Isn't this wonderful?" But I didn't dare, because of pride coming before a fall.

We turned together round the red flag standing alone in a field of plough. We galloped together towards the in and out. "Steady," shouted Andrew. "Slow down a little. Steady." The next moment we were over and galloping towards the final gates. We must clear them,

I thought; we must keep level. We were so close together now that our knees knocked. We were all equally determined to jump a clear round. We'll win if we do, I thought, and then we had reached the gates. We increased our pace and the three horses rose into the air like one and we were over with inches to spare and galloping towards the finishing post, while we could hear people cheering on all sides.

"Oh, it was a marvellous round," shouted Kate, running towards us as we drew rein. Mummy and Daddy were approaching too. All our supporters seemed around us. Mr. Day was slapping Andrew on the back and crying: "Well done, my boy. You've shown people something."

Laurence and I dismounted and grinned at one another.

"That was a brilliant display," said Daddy, patting Daystar in a way which tells knowing people that he isn't horsy.

"You kept beautifully together," Mummy told us.

"You're easily the best," Daddy said.

Valentine was jubilant, Harry madly excited. Mrs. Day stroked Mulligatawny's nose and said: "Oh, you good thing, you good thing."

I thought how dreadful it would be if we hadn't won; after everyone's congratulations and the cheers of our supporters.

More people were loading their horses into boxes. Some of them had only just finished competing.

"Well, you've beaten the shires to-day," said Mr. Day.

"Don't speak too soon," cried Kate.

"Go on with you," cried Mr. Day. "The Chill Valley Hunt have won and you know it."

"I wish they would hurry up and give the results," cried Kate. "I can't bear this suspense much longer."

"But there's still a three going round," said Valentine.

"Do the judges take matching horses into consideration?" inquired Daddy anxiously. "If so they may put you down on that. I mean, you don't match very well, do you?"

"We didn't tell them to," answered Valentine.

"Anyway, we could be worse," I said. "I don't think two dark horses with a grey in the middle are a very badly-matched three."

"I'm sure they're not counting looks," said Andrew. "If they were, they would have had us all parading round them first."

"They would have looked at clothes, too," said Valentine. "Wouldn't Mr. Watson have been in his element?"

"Oh, I do wish they'd hurry up," said Kate, looking longingly towards the judges' wagon.

"Patience, Kate, patience," remarked Mrs. Day.

"And now I have the results of the last class," announced Colonel Hayward. "Class Five." Kate started to skip about like someone possessed. I bit my nails frantically. Valentine tightened Mulligatawny's girths. Laurence put his hands in his pockets and took them out again. Andrew looked away from us all pretending he didn't care. Daddy blew his nose. "The prize to be awarded for the best round done by any three representatives from any hunt," continued Colonel Hayward.

"Oh, do hurry up," shrieked Kate.

"Ssh, do be quiet," said Mrs. Day.

"First prize goes to the Chill Valley Hunt," announced Colonel Hayward with an unmistakable note of triumph in his voice.

"Hurray, hurray," shrieked Kate.

"I said you had," cried Valentine.

"Well done, Andrew. Good old Andrew," yelled Harry.

"Up with the Chill Valley Hunt," cried Mr. Day.

"Well done," said Daddy.

"That's wonderful," said Mummy.

It's true, I thought. We really have won, I'm not just dreaming; and I don't care how much horrible people complain, I'm glad.

Someone legged me up; and I felt as though I had won the Grand National as we cantered across to the judges' wagon. The sun was shining. It was one of those wonderful spring evenings one never forgets. The horses cantered beautifully together. Behind us was the team from the shires—three men on three chestnuts, all beautifully turned out. The three which had won third had already left for home, so they would have their prizes posted to them.

"I never thought we'd do it," said Andrew, smiling happily. "Not after I saw your last two efforts round the course."

"Our horses like going together; don't they, Sandy?" said Laurence, and I agreed.

"Well done, the Chill Valley Hunt," said Major Sunderland as he handed Andrew, Laurence and me our red rosettes. "I've never seen a three keep together better than you did. It was an amazing performance."

"You must have worked a lot," said Mr. Peterson.

"Your girths are loose, Sandy," said Mr. Watson, smiling from behind the judges' backs.

I ignored my loose girths and we cantered back to the starting post with our rosettes between our teeth. Colonel Hayward and Felicity and Patience congratulated us, and we all dismounted; and Andrew and Laurence thanked Colonel Hayward at some length for being such an able starter and for lending us Melcham for the day. Colonel Hayward said: "Not at all, it's a pleasure to be of some assistance, and I'm glad you've done so well." Then he and Andrew and Laurence disappeared in search of the judges, leaving Felicity, Patience and me with the horses.

"You have done well," said Patience, patting Mulligatawny. "I should love to ride in hunter trials."

"We might have some for people under twenty-one in the autumn," I said, forgetting that the hunt might not exist then.

"Oh, that would be lovely," cried the Haywards.

Kate passed us in the landrover. Mr. Day was driving. "We're going round to pick up the flags," she shouted, waving madly.

"I do like the Days," said Patience. "Especially Kate."

Valentine was helping Mummy pack up the contents of the secretary's tent. Nearly all the horse-boxes had left. A few people were still drinking cups of tea and beer in the refreshment tents.

"You must have made lots of money," said Patience. "What are you going to spend it on?"

I remembered our reason for holding the hunter trials. But I couldn't tell Patience the truth. "We haven't decided yet," I lied.

Valentine came across. "The secretary's tent is dismantled," she said. "It's now reclining in the back of your car."

"That's wonderful," I said.

Andrew and Laurence were shaking hands with the judges. The last horse-box was leaving.

"Sixty-seven cars," said Mr. Mitchell, suddenly beside us. "I've handed the money in at the tent."

"And there were some beauties, too," said Sid. "Three Rolls; and a couple of Bentleys, new this year by the look of them."

"You've made something to-day, haven't you?" said Mr. Mitchell. "You'll be getting a Rolls yourselves, soon."

"I doubt it," I said. "Though a Rolls would be very useful to the hunt. We could hire it out for weddings and make money that way."

Laurence and Andrew had collected their horses from the Haywards and were mounting. We all thanked Mr. Mitchell and Sid for watching the gate, several times. Then Kate appeared with Dusty and we rode away from Melcham with the sun shining on our backs.

None of us spoke until we reached the road. Then we all started to talk at once. At first, we each related our exact feelings as we had ridden round the course. But later, when we turned down the quiet country road which would lead us to Allate, Laurence said: "I suppose everyone heard the remarks going around this afternoon?"

Andrew said: "We could hardly avoid it."

"We weren't meant to," said Valentine.

"Horrid jealous beasts!" exclaimed Kate.

"Of course, we were asking for trouble," said Laurence, "We shouldn't have given the judges lunch."

"According to most of them, we shouldn't have entered either," said Kate angrily.

"But surely people always enter in their own hunter trials?" said Valentine. "They're not like shows."

"They become more so every day," said Andrew.

"But did any of you hear the doting daddy's prize remark?" asked Laurence. "It was just after Kate won the children's class. Do you know he said: 'That child's Major Sunderland's niece, and Mr. Peterson's her godfather.' He did, honestly."

We all laughed and I began to feel more cheerful. Kate repeated the unpleasant remarks she and I had overheard, and Andrew said that he had heard the judges were to stay at Long Chill Farm over the weekend. We all began to giggle then and we became very silly. We prepared rooms for them in our imagination, and cooked a huge breakfast of bacon and eggs and a dinner of five courses. We laughed until Kate was crying and all our sides were aching.

"Anyway, we've made lots of money," cried Kate finally. "And we need never hold hunter trials again."

"It's our reputation I'm worried about," said Laurence suddenly serious again.

"But have we one, except perhaps as the maddest, baddest pack of hounds in England?" I cried.

"I hope so," said Laurence. "Or we'll never be recognised."

The Days remained silent, and I guessed that they were thinking, what does our reputation matter, when soon the hunt will be no more?

"What we need to do," I said, "is to go right into our critics' country and beat them at their own hunter trials."

As I spoke, I was jumping as a team again, abreast with Andrew and Laurence, our horses taking off together and landing together, clearing fence after fence.

"Yes," cried Kate enthusiastically. "That's a super idea. That would really settle the matter."

"But are there any hunter trials between now and the autumn?" asked Laurence.

"A few, I think," said Andrew. "Though it's getting late for them."

"There aren't any near, I know," said Valentine. "We'd have to box and that'll cost money."

I decided to say no more on the subject, but I was determined to find some hunter trials where we could compete with the people we had ridden against to-day, and, I hoped, win.

Allate was full of the peace of a spring evening. Long shafts of sunlight lay across the green; the trees stood gold against the setting sun. In the cottage gardens the villagers were digging and planting; on the lawns there were daffodils. And, as we passed the bakery, still smelling faintly of new bread, and took the path which would lead us down into the valley, I suddenly felt weary, too weary to talk any more. To me then, the future seemed fraught with difficulties. Our victories of the day seemed nothing when compared with the tragedy we were fighting. Quite suddenly the hunt ball became a giant undertaking. All our enterprises have been on too large a scale, I thought. If only we could have started by holding small hunter trials for local people under twenty-one, and a little friendly hunt ball with five pound tickets. I foresaw hundreds of dissatisfied people on Friday night, complaining that the band was too loud, the food not good enough, and the organisers mere kids dressed as grown-ups. The past seemed like paradise to me then; filled with small activities like exercising hounds for the first time, carpentering, converting farm buildings into kennels, cooking puddings for hounds. I forgot that there had always been days when the future had looked stormy, but that somehow our troubles had always come right in the end.

"We must have made a fair whack today," said Laurence. "Over a thousand pounds, I should think."

"I hope the hunt ball does as well," said Valentine.

We talked about our horses as we neared the valley; each of us held forth on the merits of our own.

"One day Overture will shake the hunter trial world," said Laurence. "A little more schooling . . ."

"Dusty never faltered," Kate said. "Not once the whole way round."

I patted Daystar. "She was marvellous," I said.

"I bet Overture could win a point-to-point," said Laurence. "She's so fast and she's got so much scope; she would gain over every jump."

Andrew patted Mulligatawny. "I'm afraid we'll have to start advertising ours soon," he said. And I knew he meant their horses and gloom descended suddenly on us all.

"Surely you needn't sell them till nearer the autumn?" Laurence said as we reached flat land again and saw the lights of Long Chill Farm welcoming us through the twilight. "Hunters always fetch more later in the year."

"But the auction's on August the eighteenth," said Andrew, "and they must have gone by then."

Laurence fell silent. Far away, I could hear the clanging, thumping noise of an express train on its way to London.

"Well, I should wait a little longer," said Laurence. "I shouldn't be rushed into anything."

Andrew grinned without mirth into the dusk. "It's difficult to rush a Day," he said. "But I'll remember."

Mrs. Day's ducks were still on the pond by the yard gate. They looked whiter than usual in the twilight. Laurence and I said good night to the Days as they turned towards the stables, and we arranged to meet them on the morrow to discuss the hunt ball.

"Were there ever such pessimists as the Days?" asked Laurence when we were on the track for home. "If only they would do something to help themselves,"

"I can't bear to think about that any more," I cried. "They're all so hopelessly dreary nowadays; they're quite different from what they used to be when we first started our pack."

Lost Horizon was galloping round the paddock. Soon she'll be competing in hunter trials, I thought.

"We'll win through yet," said Laurence, still talking about the Days and the hunt. "It won't be long now before we have money behind us and that will be a tremendous help."

I thought that Laurence was as much an optimist today as the Days were pessimists, but I didn't say so.

In Little Hall our parents were opening a bottle of red wine to celebrate Laurence's and mine and the Hunt's successes during the day.

SEVEN

Gloom followed the hunter trials. The Days talked again of advertising their horses, and Mr. Day actually sold his aged roan hunter, Pink Gin, to a neighbouring farmer.

Laurence was still determined on victory; if he ever doubted it he let none of us know. He refused to discuss ways and means of disposing of our pack, and he continued to talk of next season as if life was to go on as it had before. The Days nicknamed him the Mad Optimist; and, though they worked hard on the preparations for the hunt ball, they did so without enthusiasm.

I felt pessimistic about the future of the hunt. But, still stinging from the remarks I had overheard on Saturday, I was determined to find some hunter trials where we could ride against our critics, and, I hoped, beat them. While I prepared frantically for the ball—even so far as visiting London with Mummy and buying a dress, which was strapless and gold and white—my thoughts were at hunter trials.

Valentine supervised the arrangements in the ballroom. We, or rather our guests, were to dance by candlelight; there would be a buffet in the dining-room; a separate disco; and space for sitting out in the hall. Still dreaming of the hunter trials, I agreed to everything suggested. I consented to wearing flowers in my hair at the ball, and a choker necklace round my neck, and to having my hair shampooed and blow-dried—for the first time in my life—on Friday afternoon. I looked forward to Saturday and to the arrival of *Horse and Hound*, perhaps with an advertisement of hunter trials inside, far more than to dancing by candlelight in my new evening dress.

Laurence and I and the Days took frantic dancing lessons in order to partner wealthy subscribers too aged to brave the disco. The establishment we visited was Miss Blake's School of Ballroom Dancing. We suffered agonies in a basement room, while a cassette played modern dance tunes and a plump blonde, who had adenoids, gave languid instructions and danced with each of us in turn. We dreaded the approaching ball more after each visit to Miss Blake's Dancing School; our only consolation was the journey home in the bus. For then, so pleased were we to have left another lesson behind us that we became madly cheerful. The Days forgot their sorrows, and we imitated our blonde teacher, until the rattling country bus reached Allate and the conductor, who knew us all quite well, yelled: "Where are you going to? Timbuctoo?"

Valentine acquired a new dress, and Kate borrowed one from a distant cousin. Andrew and Laurence were in despair about their dress clothes. Neither could borrow from their father, because Mr. Day and Daddy had both bought tickets for the ball and showed every intention of using them. And anyway, as Valentine said, they would only be correctly attired in scarlet.

Then Daddy produced the perfect solution. "Go to Moss Bros. and hire evening clothes," he told Laurence.

Laurence and Andrew became mad with joy, and next day, Laurence wearing his boring brown suit and Andrew in corduroy trousers and a hacking coat, they departed to London in search of Moss Bros. and hunt evening dress.

Valentine ordered mountains of flowers. She wouldn't say how much they were to cost; I guessed twenty-five pounds, but from the way she looked at me I knew they must be costing nearer fifty. We arranged them on the Friday morning before the ball. Thursday evening had seen our last dancing lesson. The blonde had been more friendly. At first we thought because she was so pleased to be losing such unpromising pupils. But later, we changed our minds. I danced with Andrew first on this occasion. We danced a foxtrot and then a waltz and he trod on my right toes five times and my left toes eleven times, and I kicked his shins at every corner. However, Valentine and Laurence did better. They really looked quite natural dancing together, except for Laurence's right arm appearing peculiarly stiff and Valentine's expression portraying a mixture of agony and concentration. Poor Kate, dancing with our blonde instructress, was frantically watching her feet and muttering the steps to herself as she waltzed round the room. When the waltz finished the blonde changed the cassette.

Andrew mopped his brow and Valentine grinned, and Laurence said: "You know, I do believe we're beginning to get it at last."

"I wish I was," said Kate.

"You must practise skipping," said the blonde. "That should make you lighter on your feet. And try to walk better with your head up and your chest out. Think, I'm Miss Day and I want all the world to know it."

I didn't dare look at Laurence and the Days. I didn't want to giggle. Already, I could hear us imitating our instructress in the bus on our way home.

"Wake up, sleepy," cried the blonde. "I'm dancing this with you."

She seized me in an iron grasp and we began to dance. The room felt suffocatingly hot. "Quick, quick, slow, quick, quick, slow," she said and I shuffled round unable to see beyond her shoulder—she was tall as well as plump—and longing for the lesson to end. "You're not doing so badly," she told me. "You ought to try for the bronze medal. A dozen more lessons and you would pass easily." In spite of the iron grasp I shuddered. "Quick, quick, slow, quick, slow," continued the blonde. "Steady, you're pulling me round. Don't be so headstrong. No man likes to be organised. Try and go with me. Quick, quick, slow." I wasn't sure whether I was meant to be dancing a waltz or a quickstep. I frantically did heel turns whenever the blonde tightened her grasp and she said: "You'll need several more lessons before you'll be ready to dance at a ball. Don't rush so; remember you'll be wearing a long dress."

My heart sank. We seemed to have endured a multitude of lessons already. Surely, soon, I would be able to dance? I didn't dare admit that the ball we were preparing for was actually to take place during the next forty-eight hours. I decided that I would hide in the disco and would refuse every dance, wealthy subscribers or not, and that our lessons had been a waste of money we could ill spare. At last the cassette ended and the blonde started it again and danced with Laurence. I stood and watched until told to practise on my own, paying particular attention to my heel turns. I thought how wonderful life would seem when the ball was over, and if we found some hunter trials in the weeks ahead.

Travelling home later in the bus, none of us laughed as much as usual. Kate and I had pretended to be important as we walked through Chidlington, but Valentine didn't seem to find it funny. She said: "Don't be silly," and "She's quite right, we do walk badly. We all need lessons in deportment." I decided that Valentine was becoming horribly grown-up and definitely affected.

In the bus Laurence and Andrew laughed and talked together about their day in London.

Kate said: "I don't mean to dance one single dance tomorrow night. We should have just had a disco."

And Laurence and Valentine, who I believe had actually enjoyed the lesson, said: "Don't be silly. You *must* dance," and "Hunt balls are hunt balls."

I remained silent, but determined to disappear from the ball at the earliest possible moment.

Arranging the flowers was not much fun. Kate and I spent ages putting yellow and white ones into a glass vase, but when we had finished Valentine said they looked awful and took them all out again. After that we only filled vases with water, carried them to their appointed positions, and handed Valentine scissors when she looked as though she wanted them.

After lunch Mummy drove me into Chidlington to have my hair done. "You really must have it permed soon," she said, brutally depositing me on the doorstep of a cream building called La Maison Jane.

Fortunately, quite a nice girl took charge of me. I soon discovered that she rode, and we discussed horses.

I emerged in an hour's time with my hair clean and vaguely wavy and my head still suffering from the effect of the blow-drier. I was instantly hailed by a voice which I recognised, after a moment's thought, as belonging to David Peterborough. I looked across Chidlington's ancient and historic High Street and saw him standing outside the saddler's shop with a saddle under one arm. He crossed the road and I noticed that he was wearing corduroy trousers and a dark-coloured hacking jacket. In spite of such informal clothes, he still looked immaculate.

"Hallo, how are things?" he asked. "I meant to congratulate you on your hunter trials on Saturday, but I didn't get a chance. I thought they were first class."

"We didn't think so," I said, feeling glad that at least one person had enjoyed them. "We thought they were rather a flop really." I tried to sound off-hand, but I suspect I only succeeded in sounding miserable.

"But why?" asked David Peterborough, his face expressing amazement. "You did awfully well."

"That's just the point," I answered. "I wish we hadn't."

"I know what you mean," he answered, suddenly smiling. "You mustn't pay any attention to those sort of remarks. There are always people who complain if they don't win at every show and at every hunter trials, whoever's judging."

"But their remarks were so horrid," I cried. "As if we would have practised over the course before the day; or have given the judges lunch to influence their decisions in our favour. It never dawned on any of us that people could be so beastly. However, we mean to show them." I began to reveal my plans to David Peterborough.

Looking up and down the High Street, he asked: "Have you time for a cup of tea? There's quite a decent place just across the road."

I looked at my watch. I wanted to catch the four-thirty bus home and it was now four o'clock. A few minutes later I was drinking tea and eating home-made bread, butter and honey, in a shop called The Country Kitchen. I told David Peterborough of my plan for us to compete in hunter trials somewhere not too far away in order to show the world that we *could* do good rounds over any course anywhere. Then, because he seemed sympathetic and because I knew he cared about the hunt, I told him all our troubles—how we were fighting to save our pack, how time was short, and how terrible the future was to be if Long Chill Farm and the kennels were sold to a stranger and there were no longer the Days and a pack of hounds in the farm across the valley from Little Hall. He looked grave while I was talking, but when I finished he only said: "But we can't let this happen. The Chill Valley Hunt must go on," which, of course, I knew. I was disappointed. I don't know what I had expected him to say. Already, I wished that I hadn't said so much. I felt a traitor to the hunt—to the Days and Laurence. David Peterborough lit a cigarette and blew curls of smoke towards the ceiling.

"It's secret, of course," I said, and then, "I really must be going now. Thank you very much for the lovely tea."

"Obviously it's secret," said David Peterborough. "But don't go yet. I think I can help you with the hunter trials, even if I can't save the hunt just at this moment."

I sat down again and he poured us each another cup of tea. Then he said: "There's going to be a show and hunter trials quite near where I live at the beginning of next month. The Chill Valley Hunt will count as an adjacent pack, I'll see to that, and there's a pairs class as well as an open."

"But that's wonderful," I cried, thinking there's still the money for the horse-box to find.

"I shall be able to put your horses up for you the night before," said David Peterborough, seeming to read my thoughts. "Most of my horses are out or will be by then, so I'll have plenty of room."

I could hardly speak for joy. Surely the Days will be pleased now, I thought, thanking David Peterborough at least three times, "You'd better ring me about it nearer the day," he said. "The date should be in *Horse and Hound* tomorrow. I should get a schedule as soon as you can, so as to get your entries in before they close."

I thanked him for the tea again and then, because it was twenty-five past four and the nearest bus stop was nearly a quarter of a mile away, I dashed out of The Country Kitchen. And I ran straight into Mr. Austin Smith.

"Hallo, are you going to be the belle of the ball to-night?" he cried. "How's the mare?"

"Grand," I shouted. "She'll soon be able to compete in hunter trials." And then, shouting, "I've got to catch a bus," I ran away down the High Street.

I thought about the hunter trials all the way home. I decided that Kate and I must practise a great deal together and win the pairs class. I wondered whether David Peterborough's stables were very smart; I knew he had at least one groom.

On arriving home I was greeted by a radiant Laurence. "We've both hired the most super outfits," he cried. "You've no idea how smart we look in them. Honestly, you'll have a fit when you see us, everyone will. Gosh, your hair looks different, much cleaner. I never knew it was that colour. It's positively fair."

I'd never known Laurence so excited before. "I expect it's the muck they put on it," I said, alluding to my hair.

"Someone's special rinse." said Laurence, laughing.

I was dying to tell him about my encounter with David Peterborough, but he would only be funny about clothes and tease me about my hair. He rushed round the house singing songs from *Cats* and *Top of the Pops*.

"We had a wonderful day in London," he told me. "Lunch in a pub and tea on the train coming back. Andrew was in marvellous form and we hardly stopped laughing the whole way home."

"Sounds a terrible expedition to me," said Mummy.

"And Moss Bros. was full of simply fantastic clothes," said Laurence. "They let us go all over the shop, poking our noses in everywhere. And the tack! I could have spent a thousand pounds in five minutes."

Later I managed to tell him my news. His response was disappointing. "But that's marvellous," he said, and, "How nice of David Peterborough." But it was obvious that his mind was elsewhere. I decided to impress the facts on him again after the ball.

We had an early dinner. Then we started to dress, which wasn't as easy as it sounds. First there was a traffic jam outside the bathroom door; next, there were cries from Laurence when he came to tying his white tie; and there were screams from Daddy, because his cuff-links were missing from their box on the dressing-table. Daddy tied Laurence's tie and Mummy found the cuff-links in another shirt of Daddy's. Then I put my new dress on the wrong way round and couldn't get it off again, and Laurence found he hadn't a clean handkerchief, and Daddy discovered that his evening shoes were dusty. Mummy helped me out of my dress and blew the dust off the evening shoes. Daddy lent Laurence a handkerchief. After that, I brushed my hair for three minutes without stopping—I timed myself—which apparently, according to Mummy is an idiotic thing to do just after you've had it done? Daddy found one of his evening socks had a hole in it and Mummy said if we didn't all show more sense she would be in a lunatic asylum before morning. In spite of all this, we were dressed by ten to eight and, since the ball didn't begin until nine, there was nothing we could do but stand about until it was time to leave.

Laurence looked marvellous in scarlet hunt evening-dress; he actually looked his age, and at first glance, he might even be taken for twenty. Mummy was wearing black velvet; Daddy looked unfamiliar in tails.

I was wearing the flowers, specially bought for the occasion, in my hair, and Mummy's amber beads round my neck. I tried to remember the steps of a quickstep, but now that I was no longer in the presence of the blonde, I could only recall, "Quick, quick, slow; quick, quick, slow," which buzzed in my head unceasingly. None of us felt like talking. Mummy looked at a fashion magazine; Laurence drew back the curtains and gazed out of the window; I looked at my dress and wished that I could have spent the money it cost on a lovely thick underblanket with red stripes for Daystar. The next ten minutes passed incredibly slowly.

Then Laurence drew the curtains again and said: "Do you mind if we go now? There may be things to arrange when we get there, and I must be present as the hour strikes."

The night was moonlit and very still. I felt like another person stepping into the car with a cape of Mummy's over my shoulders and flowers in my hair.

We left Little Hall, looking smaller than usual in the moonlight and I thought of our return in the cold grey light of the morning. It seemed incredible that I should soon be among a crowd of people in a candlelit room, attending my first, and our own, hunt ball. Our parents discussed the friends they were likely to meet during the evening as Daddy drove. Laurence and I were silent.

The miles slid by all too quickly. Soon we could see the club, long, low and rambling, superbly romantic in the moonlight. Outside was parked a Bentley and the Days' landrover.

"I love this place," said Mummy. "I really think we ought to belong."

"The entrance fee's three hundred pounds," said Daddy, as though that settled the matter.

We could hear the band tuning up as we stepped out of the car into the crisp evening air. Somewhere an owl hooted. Beyond the club were tennis courts and, farther away, the river.

"What a heavenly night," said Mummy. She and I stood on the steps outside the front door, while Daddy and Laurence parked the car. The air smelt of flowers, of the river, and of spring.

The Days greeted our arrival with great enthusiasm. They all seemed excited and looked quite unlike their usual selves, in evening-dress. Kate was wearing blue, and a red snood in her dark hair; Mrs. Day was in grey, which I didn't think suited her at all; Mr. Day was magnificent in scarlet and Valentine looked tall and twentyish in a checked dress. Andrew was wearing the clothes he had hired from Moss Bros. and between his coat buttons he carried his horn, which was unusually clean and shiny.

"Come and look at the ballroom," cried Valentine.

"We thought you were never arriving," said Kate. "We imagined all sorts of awful things like car smashes."

"But we're more than twenty minutes early," said Laurence.

"You know how Kate panics," said Andrew.

I must say the ballroom really did look lovely. The

candles gave out soft light, and the panelled walls and the polished floor reflected it. The flowers arranged by Valentine added a touch of colour and gaiety to the scene, and the red velvet curtains at the windows gave the room an air of expensive luxury.

"Almost too dignified for a ball," was Daddy's comment.

"But the chandeliers," I said, looking upwards to where they hung from the ceiling. "They're frightfully frivolous."

"I feel we're dressed all wrong," said Kate. "Shouldn't we be wearing crinolines?"

"Everything's ready," said Valentine. "Come and see the buffet."

In the dining-room a long table was piled high with food: chicken and lobsters; ham and legs of mutton; huge cauldrons of soup; salads, mushrooms, asparagus, smoked and fresh salmon; potato mayonnaise; vast quantities of toast and bread rolls and biscuits, and butter; lashings of whipped cream; meringues; gigantic bowls of trifle; lemon pie; strawberry flan; urns of coffee. Behind it all stood a chef in a white hat.

"There're five different kinds of ices in the fridge," said Kate.

"There'll be soup and chipolatas at the end of the ball," said Valentine. "When the clock strikes three and everyone suddenly feels limp."

"It's a stupendous display," said Laurence. "Never have I seen so much food before."

The chef smiled. Behind him were ranged rows and rows of bottles, everything from champagne to red and white *Vin de Table*.

"Well, don't begin now," said Andrew. "There'll be plenty of time to eat before another day begins. I say, Sandy," he continued, "you do look great."

"I don't feel it," I said, looking at my fashionable shoes. "I would give anything to be in hunting kit."

"Same here," said Kate.

"Don't be so unsophisticated," said Valentine. "I can see you both developing into hard-faced hunting bores."

"With hair-nets," said Kate. "Like those two unpleasant women at the hunter trials."

"Its five to nine. Don't you think you had better take up your position, Laurence?" Andrew said.

All our parents had vanished together.

Laurence stood by the entrance waiting for the first guests to arrive. The hall porter was ready to take their tickets and to announce their names; but there was no sign of any of our guests.

"Oh, how I hate waiting," sighed Laurence as ten minutes passed.

"Surely someone will arrive soon," said Kate.

The optimism I had felt on entering the ballroom, slowly died in me. I saw half a dozen couples, in my imagination, dancing silently in the candlelight; I saw the mountains of food going back to wherever it came from uneaten; I heard Valentine's and Laurence's remarks afterwards in the cold grey light of dawn; and I already felt the feeling of helplessness which would come over us when we knew that our ball had flopped. I saw bills for pounds we could not pay and then, suddenly, I realised that we had sold more than a hundred and fifty tickets in advance for twenty pounds each, so whatever happened we still had plenty of money in the bank.

"No one ever arrives on time for a ball," said Valentine. "It's not fashionable. We'll be lucky if we have a dozen people here before ten."

"Well, what on earth am I standing here for, then?" demanded Laurence. "I'm getting horribly cold leaning against this particularly icy pillar. Soon I shall turn into a pillar myself and then what will our guests say?"

"You can't be as cold as I am in my strapless evening-dress," I said.

"Well, there's no need for you to wait here," said Laurence unsympathetically. "Why don't you go into the ballroom and wait in the warm?"

"I couldn't bear to," I replied. "The band might start up, expecting me to dance."

"What, by yourself?" asked Laurence, laughing.

"Besides, I want to see the first people arrive," I added.

"I say, isn't anyone coming?" asked Daddy, appearing from the direction of the bar. "It's twenty-past nine and I haven't seen a soul."

"Apparently people don't appear until ten," said Laurence. "It's the fashion."

"How perfectly ridiculous," said Daddy. "They should come at the time advertised."

He drifted away again and Valentine said: "I like your father in tails; they make him look taller."

"He's quite tall enough anyway," I said. "He'd need a sixteen-two horse if he hunted."

"Gosh, I do feel awful," said Kate. "I think I'm going to be sick."

"Don't be silly," said Valentine. "I've never known

anyone fuss so much about a ball."

"I hear a car," cried Andrew.

"Ssh," said Valentine. "Why don't some of you go into the ballroom? You look so silly all standing round Laurence."

My brother stood up very straight; he flipped the scarlet tails to his coat, straightened his tie and smoothed down his hair. "Do I look twenty-five, or still only eighteen?" he asked.

"Mr. Watson, Mrs. Watson and Miss Smellett," announced the hall porter in a pompous voice.

Kate gave a nervous giggle. Laurence shook them all by the hand. In spite of his dinner jacket, Mr. Watson looked much the same as usual. Soon he was talking to us.

"Hiring this place must have cost you a pretty penny," he said, looking us up and down. "Of course, there's not many places big enough for a ball of this sort. I'm surprised to see you all turned out so well. Did you hire from Moss Bros. for the occasion?"

Laurence gave a start; a look of anguish crossed his face; then he stared furiously at the pillar behind him. I must say I did think Mr. Watson's remark was particularly tactless—I don't believe he ever thinks twice before he speaks. Laurence has always been touchy about clothes and anyway no one wants people to know when they've hired their clothes.

Mr. Watson didn't seem to notice that none of us had answered his question. Soon he was talking about the hunt: how we must be quite rich by now; how we were becoming very smart, and how well we had done at the hunter trials.

We were all hoping to catch a second glimpse of Mrs. Watson, whom we had never seen before. At last she emerged from depositing her coat and we saw that she was small with grey hair and a nice face. Miss Smellett, who was tall and looked cross, emerged with her and the three of them vanished towards the ballroom.

"Some of us really must go and dance soon," said Valentine.

Colonel and Mrs. Hayward arrived next with their party. They were very jovial. At least Colonel Hayward was; he insisted on shaking us all by the hand and said: "This is a very fine setting, a very fine setting indeed." But soon he and his party disappeared into the ballroom and Kate said: Oh, I *do* wish some more people would come and looked longingly towards the entrance. "Why must they be so late?"

Somewhere a clock chimed the half-hour.

"Never has time passed so slowly," exclaimed Laurence.

I shivered.

"Why on earth don't you go and wait where it's warm?" my brother asked again in a exasperated voice.

A cold draught was blowing in through the entrance. I made no answer. I wouldn't admit that I couldn't bear to go alone to the ballroom and the Days showed no intention of leaving Laurence. Soon my teeth were chattering and Kate said: "Why don't you get your coat?"

Another party arrived and then another. The band started to play. "Let's dance," Valentine suggested to Andrew.

"Too early" he answered.

Mr. Austin Smith arrived with an enormous and already hilarious party. He cried: "*Fair girls and grey horses*," and immediately introduced his guests to Kate and me, calling us "the gallant whips." I could think of little to say and Kate seemed struck completely dumb. The women all wore exotic coats and smelt of scent, and the men were hearty and laughed loudly all the time. "That's grand," they said, or "For'ard away."

"Whips! but how wonderful!" the women said, turning to one another. "Don't you think that's marvellous?"

Laurence talked politely to Mr. Austin Smith. The band had started to play. Outside another car was depositing its passengers on the doorstep. Mr. Austin Smith shepherded his large party away.

"Shall we go and see what's happening?" asked Andrew, looking towards the ballroom. "Do you mind if we desert you, Laurence?"

"Of course not," answered Laurence. "You should be introducing people to one another on the floor."

We heard the crunch of gravel as more cars drew up outside. Regular thumping beats emanated from the disco.

"Fare thee well, then," said Valentine to Laurence.

We left him shaking fresh guests by the hand. He looked dignified and very self-possessed.

"He does it awfully well," said Andrew, looking back.

There were quite a few people dancing. "Do you think the band's okay?" Valentine asked.

I'm not musical, so I couldn't really judge, but I said:

"Yes, wonderful."

Andrew said: "Shall we dance?" The band was playing a waltz—*The Blue Danube*—but it stopped before we had been on the floor any time at all. Everybody clapped rather feebly and the bandsmen mopped their brows. "That *would* happen," said Andrew.

"Bad luck," said Kate.

The next dance was a rumba and, because none of us knew the steps, we stood together in a little group watching our parents and about a dozen other people dancing. After a few minutes, Andrew said: "Why stand?" and led the way to our table, which we had chosen because of its strategic position. From it, we could watch the dining-room and the hall, as well as the ballroom.

We sat down and Andrew ordered wine, and the rumba ended. Then David Peterborough arrived with a beautiful girl wearing diamonds. His table was two away from ours and we could hear him ordering champagne.

"They'll take something in wine here tonight," said Andrew.

Laurence appeared swinging his right arm backwards and forwards. "Who would be a king?" he said. "It must be terrible shaking a thousand guests by the hand in one afternoon. I've been studying everyone's handshakes. Mr. Austin Smith's is hard and firm, he's obviously a man of determination; so's David Peterborough's. But some of them! Mr. Watson's is pretty weak. Mr. Smythe's nearly crushed my hand in two, do you think that means he's self-willed and obstinate, or merely thoughtless?"

"Both," said Valentine.

"I don't agree," said Kate.

"Does it matter?" asked Andrew.

People had already started to eat. Valentine and Laurence danced together. The ballroom was filling; soon the floor would be crowded.

"Do you think we should be introducing people?" Andrew asked me, anxiously glancing round the tables.

I followed his gaze. Nearly everyone was a stranger.

"It's not much good if we don't know their names," I said.

"I hoped you'd say that," said Andrew.

Mr. Day came to our table and said: "Everyone's delighted with everything. They say they've never been to such a ball. I told them you'd done it all. Every bit of it. Valentine, I said, she did the flowers, ordered them and all. I never had anything at all to do with it, I said. Nor my wife. It was all their own idea, I said."

Mrs. Day joined us. "You do look nice, Sandy," she said. "So does your brother. I never knew he had grown so tall."

"I wish you'd tell him that," I said, "and that you think he looks twenty-five at least. He thinks he looks about sixteen."

Mrs. Day laughed and Andrew said: "Have you had anything to eat yet?" They hadn't and they disappeared laughing towards the buffet.

"I hope what Dad says is right," said Andrew. "But I wish he wouldn't boast about us so."

The band stopped playing and Valentine and Laurence returned to the table.

"Now for dinner," said Andrew.

We ordered vast quantities of food and danced between the courses, and though I trod on everybody's toes and Andrew trod on mine, I discovered that I was enjoying myself. Kate seemed more cheerful, too. She danced twice with Laurence and a boy called Roger Wilcox who comes out hunting with us sometimes dragged her off to the disco.

The bar closed and the floor became more crowded. Andrew produced his horn and the band began to play with greater gusto.

"It's much more fun than I thought it was going to be," said Kate, eating lemon pie, meringue and ice-cream.

Valentine was dancing with Mr. Austin Smith. I watched them and wished that I could dance as well as Valentine; then suddenly I noticed Major Sunderland and his wife, and Mr. Peterson and a girl in a violet-coloured dress.

"Look," I said, pointing across to where they were sitting at a long table with fourteen or more other people.

"Ssh," said Laurence, looking discreetly. "Don't shriek so."

"Gosh!" exclaimed Kate.

"I think it's really decent of them," said Andrew. "It's a long way just for a dance."

"Do you think they're all Waynesborough people at the table?" I asked.

"I should think so," said Laurence.

I felt heartened. It was nice to think that we had friends like Major Sunderland and Mr. Peterson. I felt that they respected our pack and would stand by us in any hour of need.

"Oh, isn't this fun?" cried Kate. "I *am* enjoying myself, in spite of my awful dancing."

"So am I," said Laurence. "Much, much more than I expected."

"Same here," I said, looking beyond the candlelight, the stirring music, the gliding, shifting dancers; seeing the future, if only we raised enough money; our young puppies becoming seasoned hounds, our horses better and better schooled, our pack one of the best in England; Laurence a barrister, but still an M.F.H.; Kate a successful horse dealer; Valentine, I wasn't sure about Valentine; Andrew I saw galloping with hounds, blowing the "gone away" across autumn fields, casting our pack amidst snow-tipped hills; ageless, indomitable huntsman to the Chill Valley Foxhounds.

"Sandy!" cried Andrew. I looked up and saw Mr. Austin Smith. "May I have the pleasure of this dance?" he asked.

"He's asked three times already," Andrew hissed.

"Yes, of course," I said. "Sorry I was dreaming."

Mr. Austin Smith hardly danced at all. I said: "I'm the world's worst dancer," and he answered: "That's fine, so am I. Let's walk."

"It's being a success, isn't it?" he asked a moment later, and I guessed that he was alluding to the ball, and answered: "Yes, I think so, but I've never been to one before, so I can't really judge."

Although I didn't like dancing much, I found walking round incredibly dull and I soon fell to wishing that I was trying to dance with Andrew treading on my toes, instead of walking round with Mr. Austin Smith. At last, the band stopped playing and I said: "Thank you very much," and leaving Mr. Austin Smith, I hurried back to the table. I found the others talking to Colonel Hayward.

"Ah!" he exclaimed when he saw me. "Your turn next. I must dance with both the whips."

The band started to play again and I danced with Colonel Hayward. He didn't walk round like Mr. Austin Smith; he danced with long sweeping strides and, whenever he reached a corner, he whirled me round and round. "I hate modern dance music," he said. "There's no rhythm to it; nothing to get hold of, to make you want to dance." He whirled me round again, round and round, and I began to feel giddy and we bumped into a little fat man dancing with a tall thin woman in a powder-blue dress. "It's as bad as Piccadilly Circus," laughed Colonel Hayward.

No one seemed to be dancing the dances the blonde had taught us at Miss Blake's school of dancing. I found it difficult to follow Colonel Hayward; his whirls bore no resemblance to the heel turns, or any of the methods of turning round which I had learned during my lessons.

I was quite exhausted by the time the dance ended. I returned to our table and Colonel Hayward claimed a dance from Valentine and I collapsed in a chair and drank a cup of coffee. Later I danced with Andrew again, and I noticed how happy everyone seemed and knew that our ball was a success. Then, quite suddenly, it was two o'clock and the band became more lively. It played a Viennese waltz and Andrew whirled me round and round, even faster than Colonel Hayward had, until I hardly knew which way up I was. After that it played a Highland reel and strangers seized our hands and taught us what to do, and everyone became mad and shrieked and danced as though they would never stop. Next there came the conga and we raced round the ballroom, through the hall and up the stairs, a long, long stream of people holding on to one another.

"Oh, this is fun," shrieked Kate when I saw her. "I never knew a ball could be such fun."

Laurence had forgotten to be twenty-five any longer. His hair was on end, his tie awry. He looked about ten and seemed to be shrieking and laughing more than anyone.

Mummy and Daddy were eating at their table with their London friends. Then, as Andrew and I reached the ballroom again, the band changed to John Peel and Andrew whisked his horn from between his coat buttons and blew the gone away. After that the noise was deafening. Everyone was giving view holloas at once, and tearing round the room like maniacs. Andrew blew the gone away again and I heard someone say: "That boy's a marvel on the horn. He'd win a novice horn blowing contest."

I looked behind me and saw Major and Mrs. Sunderland and they grinned and waved. I wanted to tell Andrew what I had heard, but there wasn't time to think or speak, so fast was everyone dancing now. I hoped that it wasn't the end of the ball, though all the clocks told me plainly that it was three o'clock on Saturday morning. The gallop turned into Auld Lang Syne and everyone crossed arms and seized hands and sang at the tops of their voices. I thought, it's over, and then I thought of all the hunt balls I should be able to go to in the years to come, and I sang Auld Lang Syne louder than ever. Everyone shrieked "encore" as the band stopped playing, but instead of playing Auld Lang Syne again, it changed to God Save the Queen, and quite suddenly the ball was over.

"Now for chipolatas and soup," said Andrew. "I wonder where the others are?"

We crossed the floor and met Mummy and Daddy. "It's been a heavenly ball," Mummy said.

"Don't be too long," said Daddy. "It'll soon be light."

"We're just going to have some soup and chipolatas," said Andrew.

Gradually, we collected the others. We ate, and drank hot soup, and all the time people were congratulating us on our ball. It seemed like a dream to me, standing as I was in evening-dress for the first time. Valentine talked to the manager of the club to whom we had given free tickets for the evening. He offered us a meet of hounds any time we liked, and wished us the best of luck.

Major Sunderland shook us all by the hand before he left, and Mr. Watson waylaid Kate and asked her hundreds of questions about our money situation, our parents' ancestry and our horses' manners. Mummy appeared and said: "We're taking Mr. and Mrs. Day back, so you can all go home together in the landrover." In the ballroom, waiters were snuffing the candles and clearing the tables. Slowly, but surely, people left.

"Do you realise it's nearly four?" asked Valentine.

"Thank goodness, we haven't got to rise at six and

get ready for hunting," said Kate.

"Shall we go?" asked Laurence.

We collected our coats from yawning attendants. The band had left and, without them and the soft lights from the candles, the ballroom looked large and bleak. We wished the hall porter "good night" and found that the landrover was the only car left outside. Across the sky dawn was breaking.

"Gosh, I feel tired," said Valentine.

"Hasn't it been a success?" said Kate. "I never knew balls could be like that."

We sang on the way home. We sang *After the Ball was Over* but not the correct version. Ours was like this:

> After the ball was over
> She took out her one glass eye,
> Put her false teeth in the basin,
> Corked up her bottles of dye,
> Stood her false leg in the corner,
> Hung her false wig on the wall,
> And all that was left went to bye-byes
> After the ball.

The roads were empty; the verges of grass were glistening with dew. As we were nearing Little Hall we heard a cuckoo calling.

"Gosh, I'm looking forward to our next hunt ball," said Kate.

"So am I," said Laurence. "And I shall improve my dancing first."

I repeated to Andrew the remarks Major Sunderland

had made about his horn blowing, and though his only comment was, "People say the craziest things at that hour in the morning," he sounded pleased. Little Hall looked asleep with no lights shining out across the dim grey valley. Laurence and I wished the Days "good morning" as we stepped out of the landrover yawning and suddenly longing for sleep.

"See you after lunch," said Laurence. "We'll come down and help add up the accounts then."

A moment later, they had gone and we were climbing the stairs to bed, while across the valley we could hear the cocks at Long Chill Farm heralding another day.

EIGHT

We were all terribly dreary after the ball. Laurence wakened with a headache, and Mummy and Daddy said that the house was untidy and why couldn't we hang our coats upstairs instead of leaving them lying on the chest in the hall? I felt unusually weak. Mucking out the loose-boxes and grooming the horses seemed to take hours and hours. And by the time we had been for a ride it was tea-time.

"We'll have to let Lost Horizon have another day off today," said Laurence, as we rugged our horses. "We haven't got time to ride her now, and anyway we're both much too weak. I'm sure one buck would have me off, my legs feel like chewed string."

"I suppose we could lunge her," I said. "Or do you think she would pull us over and gallop away?"

"Most likely," said Laurence, buckling Overture's roller. "Anyway, there isn't time. It's ten to five now and we must see the Days before nightfall."

"Must we see them?" I asked.

"Yes, definitely," replied Laurence. "We can't leave money hanging about at Long Chill Farm. You know what the Days are like; it'll be muddled up with their spare cash before we know where we are."

"But surely it's mainly cheques," I said.

"Well, they've no respect for them at all," said Laurence, slamming his loose-box door. "They're probably muddled up with Kate's hunting clothes by now."

I felt cross; I didn't want to visit the Days, because I guessed that they, too, would be in bad tempers. But Laurence insisted. "We promised to go, so we've got to go," he said in virtuous accents, as we finished tea and cleared the dining-room table.

"Well, we'll never get everything settled and be back here in time for dinner," I said, looking outside to where the sun was shining on wallflowers and lilac, on green grass and the last of the daffodils.

"I'll see if I can get the car," said Laurence, disappearing towards the drawing-room, where Daddy was writing letters.

I walked out on to the terrace and looked down into the valley. The air smelt of evening, of sunshine and flowers. I wondered if we would ever have enough money to buy the kennels, and knew that if we failed, I could hardly bear to live at Little Hall any longer. The view from our windows was too bound up with our pack and with the Days; there would be no peace of mind at home without them. Each time I gazed across the familiar landscape I would imagine our pack hunting or being exercised across the valley, and, riding home at twilight through Allate, I should feel hounds around me though the familiar road would be empty.

"It's okay. We can have the car," said Laurence, suddenly beside me. "And it doesn't matter if we're late for dinner."

"That's wonderful," I said without conviction.

We drove down to Long Chill Farm with the evening sun in our faces.

"I wonder if they're in a state of collapse," said Laurence. "Thank goodness they enjoyed the ball."

"Yes, thank goodness," I said, remembering Kate's gaiety of the evening before. Already it seemed years since I was dancing by candlelight and eating smoked salmon and chicken.

We found the Days playing with the puppies. They were in the kennel yard and they shouted, "Hallo, we thought you were never coming," when they saw us.

Andrew held up Romeo and said: "Isn't he a lovely specimen?"

We sat and discussed the puppies. We carefully avoided any mention of their future and the Days seemed quite cheerful. I liked Rory the best out of the two litters. He was reddish in colour, with white on his muzzle, on the tip of his stern, and on the back of his neck in a blob the size of the old half-crown piece. Kate had fallen in love with Torchlight, the flashiest of them all. He had white round his neck, on all his legs, on half his stern and on most of his muzzle. He was cheerful and fat, and the picture of health. Laurence liked Tapestry and Rosa equally. Tapestry had an unusually serious expression for a puppy; except occasionally, when he smiled, and then his whole face became roguish. Rosa was small, with a short, square muzzle. She was light in colour; mainly white with a few patches of tan scattered carelessly on her shoulders and hindquarters.

Valentine professed a liking for the puppies no one else favoured. Andrew cared for them all equally as befitted a huntsman.

It was pleasant talking about hounds in the evening sun, but the time came when Andrew said: "I think the pups had better go in now," and we put them away with their mothers in two of the smallest lodging-rooms, which had been pigsties before we converted them. As we walked indoors, Laurence changed the conversation from hounds to money.

"Hadn't we better wind up the hunt ball accounts to-night?" he said. "I want to know exactly how much money we have made."

"Well, it isn't five hundred pounds, I can tell you that much," said Andrew.

I thought that the Days were becoming more tire-some every day. And then, quite suddenly, I remembered my piece of news—the hunter trials, which I had thought so much about and which, in the rush of the hunt ball, I had completely forgotten to mention to the Days.

Everyone was talking about money. "The club must have made quite a lot out of it. In prestige, if nothing else," said Valentine.

"The sooner we get the cheques off to the bank the better," said Laurence.

I tried to interrupt. I said: "I say——" But no one heard me.

"We still owe a lot for the oatmeal we had sent down from Scotland just after Christmas," Andrew said. "It was pretty expensive—about three pounds a hundredweight, I think."

"And Mr. Jackson wants a pound for the carcase you collected from him last week," Valentine told Andrew.

"And Daddy says we owe him money for oats," said Kate.

I wanted to cry: "Money, money, money, can't we talk about anything else?" But I restrained myself, realising that diplomacy would be necessary if the Days were to compete, as I had planned, in the hunter trials near David Peterborough's home.

We strolled indoors and Valentine produced a roll of cheques from inside a suitcase, which was hidden under a table in the hall. "Here you are," she said, handing them to Laurence. "The whole blooming lot."

"And to think that all those silly scraps of paper are as valuable as a horse like Dusty," said Kate. "Isn't it silly?"

"Ridiculous," I agreed, still longing to tell the Days about the hunter trials, but putting it off because I wanted to choose exactly the right moment.

Valentine and Laurence looked through the cheques together. Then they started to endorse them.

Kate said: "We've been in awful tempers all day. I suppose it's inevitable after a ball. Mummy and Dad are both in despair. Life is really rather awful at the moment. The trouble is, although it's obvious we'll have to leave here in August, we all keep hoping something will turn up in the meantime—like Mr. Micawber in *David Copperfield*. The result is we don't start packing and really seriously looking for jobs, and yet we can't settle down and work here like we used to. It's just miserable. Then, to make matters worse, Dad keeps saying it's time we started advertising the horses. And Andrew contradicts him and says there's no earthly reason why we should before July, and then there's a row. It's rows all the time now and there seems no point in doing anything about anything."

"And sometime we'll have to start getting rid of hounds," said Andrew, swinging round from where he had been standing and gazing out of the window.

"Yes, I know," I said calmly. Though I felt as though I was in the midst of an earthquake. "But there's still lots of time."

Andrew didn't seem to hear me. He was looking out of the window again.

"I meant to mention that our hounds would be for sale to Major Sunderland and Mr. Peterson at the ball," he said, in a miserable voice quite unlike his own. "But I was enjoying myself so much and so was everyone else, and somehow it seemed impossible to talk about it when everyone was so merry. But we can't put off the evil hour for ever. Sometime we must begin."

I saw our hounds leaving the kennels, couple by couple. Wasteful and Wishful, old friends, who had come to us from the Downshire a long time ago. Hounds we had bred ourselves and had planned to enter in August—Chill Valley Viking, Verger, Victor, Vagabond and Venus. Our two new litters, and True Love's yet to come. And worst of all, I thought of the fate which awaited Dainty and Vampire. I saw it all in my mind's eye in those few seconds while Kate and

Andrew were silent and the only noise in the hall was the scratching of Valentine's and Laurence's pens as they endorsed cheques.

Then Kate sniffed and I swung round and cried: "There's still lots of time. Weeks and weeks until August. Anything may happen. Relations may leave us thousands of pounds. The sale may be cancelled. Besides, we must be half-way towards the five thousand pounds by now. It's so feeble to give up. While there's a day left, there's hope."

"We have no rich relations," said Andrew, sounding deadly serious. "If we had we would have approached them ages ago. You always attack me, Sandy, as though I wanted the hunt to give up. You don't seem to realise that I've been into every possible way out a thousand times. If a few hundred would help us, nothing would stop me working. But it isn't enough. Twenty thousand pounds is what we need and I see absolutely no hope of getting it. We've got to leave this farm on August the eighteenth, no, the Monday before to be accurate, and that means every animal must be off the place by then. Dad is thinking of having a sale here in July, unless we manage to rent another farm during the next two months, which isn't likely, I'm afraid. So you see everything is slowly drifting to a climax and we can't just sit and do nothing much longer."

Andrew had spoken quietly and dispassionately. When he finished, another silence fell. Valentine and Laurence had stopped endorsing cheques. Outside the sun was setting beyond Badger's Copse.

"But there's still weeks before July," I said. "Can't we leave things a little longer? It would be awful if we sold our pack and then on August the eighteenth a rich millionaire bought the farm and said that you could remain there for the next twenty years. Think how awful you would feel then, with no hounds and no horses."

Valentine and Laurence had returned to their accounts.

"Two hundred and fifty pounds," said Valentine.

Their pens started to scratch again. Kate sniffed into her red-spotted handkerchief.

"Pity there aren't fairy godmothers nowadays," said Andrew.

I shall never be able to tell them about the hunter trials, I thought. They'll be miserable now for weeks and weeks.

"I answered an advertisement a day or two ago," Andrew said and I felt my heart leap with trepidation. "It was for a first whip for a pack in the West Country. Of course, I don't mean to go at once, and anyway, I don't suppose they'll answer; but I don't think there's any harm in looking round. Jobs aren't easily come by nowadays."

I didn't know what to say. None of my fears had been as bad as the news I was hearing now. Quite suddenly, the bottom seemed to be falling out of my world.

"I'm going to find a job, too," said Kate, making my heart leap again. "I shall try to get one as second horseman to an M.F.H., because I don't suppose anyone will want a girl in kennels."

"But you're too young to leave school," I cried, frantically trying to remember Kate's age.

"I shan't be soon," she replied. "My main trouble is Dusty. I want a job where I can take her, and that, of course, makes everything rather more difficult. The other difficulty is references. Do you think your father would give me one? So many of the advertisements end 'References and salary required to' etc., etc.; and I've got no idea how much people get paid and, of course, I haven't a single reference. It really makes everything very difficult."

I felt as though I was in the midst of a particularly horrible nightmare. I wished that I could waken in my bed at home and know that I had dreamed it all.

"Poor Sandy!" exclaimed Andrew. "You look thunderstruck."

"I am," I said. "I never realised that things had come to such a pass."

In my imagination I saw Andrew hunting another pack of hounds across an unfamiliar landscape, and Kate hacking a large tired hunter home along an open, windswept road.

"I think you're being very defeatist," said Laurence, who had apparently been listening while his pen scratched. "You don't seem to realise that Sandy and I are determined to keep the pack together, whatever may occur. If the farm goes, we'll move the kennels elsewhere."

"And if we go?" demanded Andrew.

"Oh, don't start quarrelling," cried Kate. "I couldn't bear it."

"I don't know," said Laurence. "We hope you won't; we can't believe you will."

"And who will look after hounds?" asked Andrew. "And where will the oats come from for the hunt horses?"

It struck me that our visit to the Days was becoming distinctly disagreeable. I remembered a saying quoted frequently by one of the mistresses at my school: *Necessity is the mother of invention.* I quoted it now.

"That's merely an excuse for escaping from reality," said Valentine.

"And you prefer to rush into it with open arms and your heads in the air," I said, suddenly feeling angry.

"Who will pay Bert Saunders to make the pudding while hounds are hunting?" demanded Andrew.

"We can make more money," said Laurence, a little wearily. "Dash it all, we've just made three hundred and fifty pounds out of our first ball, and well over a hundred out of the hunter trials. We could run two balls a year, a horse show, hunter trials, and if we become recognised, a point-to-point. The hunt could pay you to be huntsman then, Andrew, and Kate her expenses as second whipper-in."

I did some quick mental arithmetic. In fact, if hard-pressed, we could make six hundred pounds a year I decided, and with caps and subscriptions we might bring it up to a thousand.

"Packs have been run on less," I said.

"It's all a hypothesis," said Valentine.

"It's not," said Laurence. "It's hard concrete fact, and we're going ahead. We're going to get the Chill Valley Hunt recognised, and we're going to get more subscribers and more support from the whole countryside. Isn't that right, Sandy?"

I nodded. I couldn't speak. I hate quarrelling with the Days. Evening seemed to have turned into night while we had argued. I felt cold and there was a lump in my throat. Laurence and Andrew were glaring at one another. Outside on the lawn Mrs. Day was shutting up the coops. Somewhere in Allate a dog was barking as though he would never stop.

Life will be very lonely without the Days, I thought, and Laurence and I will find it terribly difficult to run the pack alone.

"We'd better go, Sandy," said Laurence. "Cheerio, everyone. We'll be down in the morning."

Outside the farm was very still. "What's the matter with them, Sandy?" Laurence asked as we drove home. "I can't understand their attitude. Sometimes I think they don't want the pack to go on."

"I think really they're in despair," I said, hearing Andrew's miserable voice again as he talked about selling hounds.

"It makes life so impossible when they won't do anything," grumbled Laurence, "Soon it'll be time to start exercising hounds again, and we ought to be visiting landowners and finding new coverts to draw next season."

"And arranging walks for the puppies," I said.

"I expect really they're just tired after the ball," said Laurence, sounding slightly more optimistic.

"I wanted to tell them about the hunter trials," I said. "But it seemed a hopeless time to choose."

"Yes, quite impossible," agreed Laurence.

The horses whinnied as we turned up the drive.

"But we must decide soon whether we're going to the hunter trials or not," said Laurence. "We can't keep Overture and Daystar stabled indefinitely."

Dinner was waiting for us in the simmering oven. I

fetched *Horse and Hound*, which had arrived during the morning, and we found the advertisement of the hunter trials. We read:

LONGWORTH HORSE SHOW AND HUNTER TRIALS
Saturday, May 12th. £600 *in Prize Money*
Open and Juvenile Jumping. Hunter and Hack Classes
Open, Pair and Novice Hunter Trials
Gymkhana Events

Further details and schedules from the Secretary (an address followed). We could not enter for the show jumping, because it was affiliated.

"Sounds all right," said Laurence.

"It looks a big enough affair, anyway," I said. "I don't think we need bother about winning too much."

"We'd better make the Days look at the advertisement tomorrow," Laurence said.

"It's the entrance money which worries me," I said.

"Well, we've still got the money we won at our hunter trials," Laurence replied. "Which must add up to quite a lot."

"Thirty pounds, as far as I'm concerned," I said. "But I meant to put it towards the kennels."

"Well, your entries won't come to that much and you may win a lot more, so I shouldn't worry," said my brother.

"I shan't win anything," I said. "But it's not really my entry fees which worry me so much. It's the Days'."

"We'll find out what they'd like to enter for," said Laurence. "And then I'll send in a cheque for the lot. If they want to know where the money's coming from, it's an advance instalment on the allowance I'm to have when I'm up at Oxford. They always think we're so well off, they won't mind."

"It'll be wonderful if we win a lot, but I know we won't," I said. "Do you think David Peterborough will be competing? He said most of his horses were out."

"I don't know," said Laurence. "He's probably still got one up. Are you going to send for a schedule or shall I?"

Finding out what the Days wanted to enter for at the Longworth hunter trials wasn't as easy as it sounds.

I told them about the hunter trials on Sunday morning, when they were all sitting in the sun watching the puppies play.

Kate cried: "How wonderful. I would love to compete," and then, collecting her thoughts, and no doubt remembering the tragedy hanging over them all, she said: "But, of course, it's impossible. We haven't any money, and we're much too busy."

"But it's not going to cost much money—only the entrance fees," I said. "That's what's so wonderful about David Peterborough's offer; and if you're short of time, Laurence and I will gladly lead your horses over the day before, won't we, Laurence?"

"Of course," said Laurence, giving me a wink.

Kate looked at Andrew uncertainly.

Valentine said: "It's very nice of you, but there's still the entry money to find."

Andrew said: "David Peterborough is behaving very handsomely."

"It *would* be fun seeing his stables," said Kate. "I bet they're smart."

Laurence began to look more hopeful. "We've written for a schedule, anyway," he said. "I don't think any of us can compete in the novice class, can we? But we might have quite a chance in the pairs, and of course, there's always the ordinary jumping classes."

"Would we hack home after the show?" asked Kate. "I mean, it's not really very far."

"That was the idea, wasn't it, Sandy?" Laurence asked.

"That's right," I said, beginning to feel excited now that the Days looked like coming. "The horses are going to sleep in at David Peterborough's, so we'll need to take rugs and things over the day before."

"We'll have to start practising tomorrow, if we're going in the pairs together, Sandy," said Kate. "We must do better this time."

"I'm determined to do well in the open," said Laurence. "I shall school and school Overture during the next fortnight, until she'll stop when I shut my little finger, and remain calm and sensible the whole way round the course."

We discussed the hunter trials for some time, and it seemed to me then that Laurence and I had won our battle, but when we took the schedule down to Long Chill Farm two days later the struggle began all over again.

"We'll be very busy on the farm then," said Andrew.

"It's the entrance money which worries me," said Valentine, looking at the schedule. "Pounds for each class. It's no joke, you know."

"But you've still got the money you won at our hunter trials," I cried. "Can't you spend that?"

"I'll lend you enough," said Laurence, "If you haven't got any. You can pay me back when you've got your super jobs and have a pay packet handed to you every Friday."

Gradually, the Days gave way. Kate became madly excited and we all entered for masses of classes, forgetting all about the entry fees. Afterwards, Laurence and I hurried home and copied out the entries tidily. Laurence wrote a cheque, and we rushed down to Allate and posted them before the Days could change their minds again.

In the evening I rang up David Peterborough and told him that we were all coming to the hunter trials. He sounded pleased. He said: "That's fine. I shall see you on the evening before, then. What time do you think you'll arrive?"

Without thinking I answered: "Tea-time," and then I felt quite overcome because I thought it sounded as though we expected to be asked to tea.

I missed David Peterborough's next words. I said: "Sorry, what did you say? I didn't hear," and he replied: "I said I hoped you would all stay to tea," and I felt worse than ever. "Won't it be an awful bore?" I asked.

"Of course not," said David Peterborough. "My mother wants to meet you all, and I love having people to tea."

"Thank you very much, then," I said.

"How many of you are coming?" he asked. "Or rather, how many horses, which is what really matters."

"Five," I said, hoping that Harry wouldn't suddenly decide to come as well. After that there seemed nothing left to say. A short silence fell and then we both said, "How are you?" at the same moment. And I laughed and David Peterborough said: "All the better for your hunt ball."

"Oh, good, I am glad," I answered.

After that there was another silence. Then we both thanked each other, said good-bye and rang off.

There were now only fifteen days left before the hunter trials. Laurence and I redoubled our schooling efforts. True Love's puppies arrived. There were nine of them and they started another of the Day v. Darlington arguments, which were becoming more frequent every day. Andrew said that nine puppies was too many for True Love to rear; he said that, much as he disliked the idea, it was his duty to knock four of them on the head, and the sooner the better.

Such a suggestion brought cries of horror from Laurence and myself. "But you can't!" I cried.

"The problem is which to kill and which to keep," said Andrew. "They're all so much alike. There isn't one which is smaller than the rest."

"But you can't possibly kill any of them," said Laurence. "They're beautiful pups. What's the point anyway?"

"That nine's too many for True Love to bring up herself," Andrew replied. "And there's no point in rearing half of them by foster mother and hand, when the hunt's not going on. But the question is, which ones are to live and which to die," he continued in miserable tones, picking up one fat puppy after another and putting it down again.

"Well, if you won't, we'll feed them by hand," I cried. "Won't we, Laurence?"

"And anyway, the hunt's not giving up," said Laurence.

Andrew continued to look miserable and to pick the puppies up and put them down again.

"What do the others think?" I asked, meaning the rest of the Days, who were not then present.

"Kate wants to keep them all and hire a foster mother and Valentine thinks we should knock three on the head, but doesn't like to say so," Andrew answered.

"Well, I agree with Kate," I cried. "I don't know how you can be so unfeeling about them."

Andrew flared up then. He said that he didn't want to kill any of the puppies, but when there was no future for the hunt what was the point of rearing them?

Laurence said that even if the hunt did give up, which was very improbable, we could always draft the puppies to another pack. I said that Laurence and I would look after the puppies, and that if Andrew would give us the address of one of the farms where we could hire a foster mother, we would gladly see to all the arrangements. Eventually Laurence and I won; Andrew wired to an address in Wales for a foster mother and Gladys managed to acquire six bottles of babies' orange juice for us to give to the puppies.

Andrew insisted on sitting up with the puppies their first night. He obstinately refused Laurence's and my offers of assistance, which infuriated Laurence. The next evening the foster mother arrived at Chidlington Station and we all dashed there together in the landrover to fetch her. She arrived in the guard's van of an express train from Wales and she was black and tan with a white ruff round her neck, and a tail which looked like a fox's brush. She smiled when she saw us and looked coy.

"Oh, isn't she sweet?" cried Kate. "Do you think we can keep her, Andrew? We really do need a dog."

"We'll have to see how things work out," Andrew answered. "At the moment, she's only hired for a month or so."

We released our puppies' foster mother from the box in which she had travelled and she shook herself and smiled again.

"I suppose she's a Welsh collie, isn't she?" asked Valentine.

"We must think of a name for her," said Kate.

We drove home through evening sunshine and, on the way, we decided to call our collie Nesta, which is a Welsh girl's name.

Nesta seemed to love True Love's puppies from the moment she saw them. She washed them endlessly and they grew larger and larger each day, and none of them died.

As May came, warm, and golden with sunshine and flowers, the Day family suddenly became madly busy. Andrew spent long hours working on the farm and had little time for anything else, even hounds. Valentine was for ever learning about computers, bringing the farm accounts up to date, or typing so many words to a minute. Kate was still at school, but in her spare time she helped her mother with the young turkeys, the goslings, the ducklings and the chicks, from dawn to dark. Poor Harry was driven hither and thither by all the family at once; one moment he was to be seen buying vast quantities of insurance stamps, the next he would be collecting the week's groceries or delivering cream, or taking a message from his father to one of the farm hands, or cutting rhubarb in the garden for lunch. The rest of his time was spent at school. He grumbled endlessly, having reached a stage when he wished only to be left in peace to collect car numbers, and play with other boys of his own age. Mr. Day was unsettled by the thought of the approaching move from Long Chill Farm to some other situation. He became absent-minded. He gave orders to his men which he contradicted a moment later; he motored into Chidlington to do the farm shopping and returned only to find that he had forgotten the most important items on his list. His temper was permanently on edge, and he seemed to have grown considerably older during the last few weeks.

Mrs. Day, already fully occupied with her poultry, insisted on spring cleaning the farmhouse and enlisting the help of Valentine and Kate whenever possible.

Laurence and I found all the Days very trying. Each morning we rode down to Long Chill Farm. We made puddings for hounds, in the two large coppers in the boiler house; we swept out the lodging rooms and washed down the courts with water. We fed the older of the puppies on minced meat, vegetables and cod liver oil, and sometimes we added orange juice, and sometimes we gave them a small amount of the pudding we had mixed for the older hounds. Most of our days seemed to be spent stirring the contents of coppers, or sweeping, until we dreamed of brooms and puddings. We badgered Andrew until he agreed to start exercising hounds again, quietly once or twice a week on foot. The first time we took them out, we lost Viking and Venus, two of our young unentered hounds. After searching half the countryside, we returned to find them ransacking the Days' kitchen. After that we were more careful. I kept my eyes glued to the pack and we all watched the young hounds vigilantly. Even so, one day Victor upset an old lady's shopping basket, and another day Venus hunted a dog across the valley.

In Allate, the orchards were gaudy with blossom. But neither Laurence nor I nor the Days had time to admire the countryside. The Days had little time for hounds, and none at all, it seemed, for practising for the approaching hunter trials. Laurence and I chose the names for True Love's puppies and the Days agreed to them without argument. The names we choose were: Raider, Raftsman, Random, Rajah, Rhapsody, Ravenous, Rouser, Ravager and Rhonda. They had to begin with R because Rambler was the father.

"We'll have to draft some hounds in the spring," Laurence told me, choosing a moment when none of the Days were near. "We're getting far too many names beginning with R, and a simply enormous pack."

Mummy and Daddy started talking about a holiday in France, but neither Laurence nor I could bear to discuss such a subject when the future of the hunt still hung in the balance. We both had the feeling that if we left the valley we would return to find the Days gone and our pack no more.

Twice we persuaded and bullied the Days into practising for the hunter trials. Both times the weather was hot and the horses jumped quietly, almost lazily, and without much interest.

And so the day before the hunter trials arrived; we washed our horses frantically before breakfast, and hoped that David Peterborough's groom would think our tack was at least reasonably clean and supple.

NINE

Laurence and I had looked at a map and found a track across fields, a path between nut trees, miles of little-used lanes, and an ancient Roman road, all of which would assist us on our way to The Limes, home of David Peterborough.

The sun was shining as Laurence and I, with egg sandwiches in our pockets, rode down into the valley. The time was twelve o'clock; the wind was in the south-east; the sky was cloudless. Everything seemed to point to a fine day.

"I hope they're ready down at the farm," said Laurence. "It's an eighteen mile ride, and we'll want a rest in the middle, for it looks like being hot."

Daystar felt fit. She jogged, and shied at a piece of paper on the ground. I felt cheerful, with the prospect of hunter trials on the morrow, and a long ride through sunlit countryside ahead of me.

Surely no one can be gloomy on such a lovely day, I thought, hoping that my companions would forget their troubles for a few hours and be as merry as they were once.

No one was ready at the farm. There were cries of horror from the stables when our horses' hoofs struck the flints in the lane.

"Oh, they are the limit," complained Laurence. "Obviously, it'll be hours before they're ready."

"Coming," shrieked Kate. "Oh, where *is* Dusty's curb chain? I shall go quite mad in a minute."

"Try your pocket," Valentine advised. Andrew came strolling out of the kitchen with his hands in his pockets.

"Hallo," he said. "You've arrived then," which seemed a particularly inane remark as we wouldn't have been in front of him if we hadn't.

I could see that Laurence was seething with impatience. He's a model of punctuality himself and he hates people to be late.

"Yes, we're here," he said, glancing at his watch, "and it's twenty-past twelve, and yesterday we agreed to be on the road by a quarter past."

"Oh, well, we generally allow too much time," Andrew answered unconcernedly. "Anyway, I don't suppose David Peterborough expects us to arrive on the dot."

Andrew disappeared into the stables and Laurence sighed.

"Well, try upstairs," we heard Valentine shout.

The next moment Kate ran past us into the house, gasping: "I can't find Dusty's curb chain anywhere. I shall never be ready."

I dismounted. "Don't you think we had better help?" I asked Laurence.

"What with?" he asked. "I'm not going to look upstairs for Dusty's curb chain."

"Harry wants to join us," said Valentine, appearing with Golden Syrup. "Do you think he can?"

It was my turn to gasp. "But he hasn't entered for anything!" I cried.

"He can make late entries," Valentine replied. "There's a pony class, which is just right for Lollipop and an under twelve jumping."

"But why on earth didn't he say he wanted to come before?" I asked. "I haven't arranged anything for him. There won't be a box ready."

I really felt rather angry with Valentine. I didn't like the idea of an extra one of us arriving at The Limes and expecting another pony to be put up; and yet I knew I should feel dreadfully mean if it was I who decided that Harry should stay behind. I felt in a horrible predicament. Laurence came to my rescue.

"It's really rather the limit," he said. "Why didn't Harry say so before if he wanted to compete?"

"Apparently no one told him that there was a show attached. He thought we were just going to hunter trials. When he saw the schedule last night he was amazed and, of course, wanted to enter," said Valentine.

"He'll be gate-crashing," I said. "I wish you had let us know last night, then we could have rung up David Peterborough and asked whether he minded an extra person."

"Oh, let him come," said Andrew, appearing on Mulligatawny. "If the Honourable David won't put up Lollipop, we can always find a farmer who will."

"I still can't find it," cried Kate, reappearing. "I've looked under my pillow (the Days have a habit of polishing their curb chains in bed) and all round the kitchen. Someone must have moved it. I know it was on Dusty's bridle last night."

"It's five and twenty-past twelve," said Laurence.

"Lollipop's frightfully fresh," cried Harry, appearing on his bouncing bay pony from the direction of the top meadow.

He hasn't even been invited to tea, I thought. I hope David Peterborough won't mind.

"Here it is in my pocket all the time," cried Kate, laughing. "I must be blind. I've been through my pockets dozens of times."

"It's half-past twelve," said Laurence in furious accents.

"You'd better hurry, Kate," said Valentine. "The Darlingtons are sick of hanging about."

At last, the Days were all mounted. We left Long Chill Farm basking in sunshine and followed the familiar path out of the valley.

"We ought to have brought the terriers," said Andrew. "Why didn't we? We are lunatics."

Much as I like Pick and Shovel, I was glad we had forgotten them. Harry, I thought, was enough of an addition without having the terriers as well. I could just imagine Pick and Shovel tearing round the Peterborough drawing-room like maniacs, running away with horses' tail bandages and generally misbehaving.

"Gosh, I'm hot!" exclaimed Kate. "I am excited about tomorrow. I wonder if the jumps for the hunter trials will be enormous. It'll be awful if they're all four feet six with enormous ditches in front."

"I wonder what David Peterborough will provide

for tea," said Harry.

"Oh, you are greedy!" exclaimed Valentine.

"I hope he gives us lardy cake like he did once before," said Kate.

Andrew handed a slip of paper to Laurence. "What do you think of that for a start?" he asked.

Somehow, I sensed that disaster lurked in that little slip of paper. I feared the worst; I decided that Andrew had found a job, or else that he had sold Mulligatawny. I looked at Kate, hoping to find consolation in her face, but she was gazing into the distance where she could see the roofs of the suburbs of Chidlington glinting in the sunlight.

Laurence handed me the slip of paper and I read: *Several couple of fifth and sixth season hounds for drafting. Also three couple unentered hounds.*

"What's it in aid of?" I heard Laurence ask.

"Of course, it's only a rough copy," said Andrew.

I looked ahead along the road, but instead of seeing the hedges on each side of us, the trees, and the shadows they cast across our path, I saw the advertisement printed in *Horse and Hound* and our fate sealed.

"You see we've got to start sometime," Andrew said, and I knew by his voice that he hated saying it.

I don't know what Laurence replied, but he and Andrew argued for the next couple of miles, casting a gloom on the beauty of the day, turning Valentine silent and Kate and me miserable.

We halted for lunch on the top of a hill, which looked down towards Chidlington where we could see the gas works, the railway lines, and the river shining and silver in the sunlight.

We loosened girths and took off bridles, so that the horses could graze in comfort. Andrew and Laurence stopped quarrelling.

Harry said: "Do you think Lollipop will win anything in the pony class?"

Kate said: "Mum and Dad are coming over to watch tomorrow."

Andrew pointed at a thick scrubby wood down below us and said: "That's a place where you'd find a fox."

I lay back on the grass and looked at the sky, so blue and cloudless. I hoped again that David Peterborough wouldn't mind an extra pony for the night and an extra person for tea. I hoped that Andrew and Laurence would stop quarrelling, and, most of all, I hoped that somehow the problems ahead of us would solve themselves.

"Do you think we'll need to get up very early tomorrow?" Kate asked.

"It depends how far the hunter trials are from The Limes," said Laurence.

"Look at those earths," said Andrew, pointing to two heaps of chalky soil farther down the hillside. "They'd take some stopping."

"I shall get up at five anyway," said Kate, "because I'm sure to lose everything."

Laurence and I ate our egg sandwiches and the Days ate boiled eggs and hunks of buttered bread. Then we bridled our horses and, mounting, we rode on.

We reached the path among the nut trees and found it overgrown. We battered our way through and when we could raise our heads again from our horses' necks, Kate found that she had scratched her forehead, Harry's nose was bleeding and Laurence had a small piece of twig in his right eye. Valentine lent Harry her handkerchief. Kate mopped her forehead rather ineffectively with her own handkerchief, and we all searched Laurence's eye for the piece of twig, until our own eyes were watering as much as his.

It was ages before Valentine found the twig, and when we started on our way again, we all knew that we would be late for tea. I don't know whether it was because of that, or just sheer incompetence which made us turn left instead of right a few minutes later. Anyway, whatever it was, after we had been riding for another quarter of an hour and all our watches told us that the time was twenty to four. Laurence looked at the miniature map he and I had made the evening before and cried: "We've gone wrong somewhere. We should be in a lane by now instead of still in the open."

I looked across the fields of young wheat, of oats and barley, in front of us and felt awful. It's bad enough arriving with an extra rider and pony, I thought, without being hours late.

"We must have turned the wrong way at the end of the nut grove," Laurence said. We had halted our horses with one accord. Now, we searched the landscape, hoping to see something familiar, some landmark which would guide as in the right direction—a wood we could remember, a river, or even just a tree. But the land we saw was unfamiliar and unpopulated, save for a few crows flying together in low formation.

Andrew cursed softly. "There's never a soul about when you want one," he said. "It's always the way."

"Shall we go on or shall we go back to the nut grove

and start again from there?" Laurence asked.

"Isn't that a road?" asked Kate, pointing to where the fields were broken by a black line, which glinted in the sunlight.

"Let's hope so," said Laurence, urging Overture forward.

We hurried our horses, but every field was sown, which meant we must ride round the headlands, which added miles to our journey. Eventually, we reached the road Kate had seen, and then we didn't know whether to turn right or left. I looked at my watch and saw that the time was a quarter-past four and I hoped frantically that the Peterboroughs had tea at five o'clock.

After a short discussion, we turned left and trotted briskly along the road.

"I shouldn't worry," said Andrew, looking at me. "I don't suppose he'll worry if we are late."

"It's his mother I'm worrying about," I said, and as I spoke, I saw an old lady with grey hair; with a shawl and lace at her wrists, with a velvet band round her neck and an ebony cane; roaming round and round an elegant drawing-room and fuming about the younger generation. "It was she who really wanted us to go to tea," I added. "She wanted to meet us, goodness knows why."

"I hope she's nice," said Kate.

"Has he a father?" asked Valentine.

"I shouldn't think so," said Laurence.

"His mother must be fearfully old," observed Kate. "I mean he's pretty old, really, thirty anyway."

"That's not old," said Andrew, "and I don't suppose his mother's much over fifty."

"I bet she is," said Kate. "I bet she's nearer seventy and old and bent and wears a pince-nez."

"And smells of lavender," said Harry.

"Ssh," said Valentine.

"What's the matter?" demanded Harry. "There's no one can hear us."

"Signpost ahead," shrieked Kate, urging Dusty faster.

"Lympton, one mile, straight ahead," she cried a moment later. "We won't be so very late after all," said Valentine. "It's only ten to five now."

Lympton is the name of the village where David Peterborough lives. I felt infinitely more cheerful as we hurried our horses on. Soon we saw houses ahead.

"Lympton," shrieked Kate. "We must be nearly there."

We passed a few new council houses with bare gardens surrounded by wire fences.

"Ugh!" cried Kate. "Why can't they plant trees?"

"And hedges," I said.

"And have gravel paths instead of concrete," said Laurence.

The sun was still shining. We came to the older part of Lympton; to cottages and to one or two Victorian houses looking too high in comparison.

"It's not nearly as nice as Allate," said Kate.

"It straggles a bit," said Harry.

Ahead I saw a white house framed by cedars, a sweep of gravel, a shady lawn, white rails and the outline of stables. I knew I had seen it before.

"Isn't that The Limes?" I cried, pointing. "It doesn't look the same as it did last time, because we're approaching it from a different angle."

"Yes, I believe you're right," said Andrew, screwing up his eyes in the face of the sun.

"Hadn't we better walk?" suggested Laurence. "We don't want to arrive on sweating horses."

We walked, and Valentine said: "It looks a jolly nice house."

Harry, who had become rather schoolified during the last few weeks, said: "Absolutely fantastic."

It's marvellous to have arrived at last, I thought, and then suddenly I remembered all that I had told David Peterborough in The Country Kitchen when we had had tea together. Supposing he starts talking about the auction, I thought, what will the Days say? They'll be furious. I wondered then why the Days were so secretive about their troubles. Andrew told me much later that it was because they hated to be the object of other people's pity.

I rode up the drive to The Limes on thorns. I remembered that I had told David Peterborough that the hunt troubles were secret, but I doubted that he would remember that now.

"There's not a weed to be seen," cried Harry. "They must have hundreds of gardeners."

"Ssh," said Valentine. "Do try and be sensible."

David Peterborough met us as we reached the house.

"Hallo," he said. "You've arrived."

"I'm terribly sorry we're so late," I said.

"We got lost," explained Kate.

"That's quite all right," said David Peterborough. "I guessed that was what had happened." He was wearing corduroy trousers and a hacking jacket. "Your horses look very well," he said. "Mine are all out at the moment. You see, I'm off to the South of France the day after to-morrow."

"Gosh, how lovely," said Kate. "Or are you going to one of those dreadful places where you parade up and down the beach all day?"

"I'm going to Cap Ferrat," said David Peterborough. "To bask in the sunshine and drink wine."

"How heavenly," said Valentine.

While we had been talking David Peterborough had been leading the way to the stables. We passed Sportsman and a couple of other horses galloping round a paddock. In another field there were jumps. Kate gave a gasp when she saw the stable yard. There was a clock tower, and grooms' quarters above the boxes which surrounded three-quarters of the yard. In the centre there was a grass lawn, where fantail pigeons fluttered in the sunlight. There were ten boxes in all, and a saddle-room.

We had all automatically halted as we passed under the clock tower.

"It was built for a trainer," said David Peterborough. "There are several good gallops a mile or so from here."

"It's a heavenly yard," said Valentine.

"Absolutely lovely," I agreed.

"It looks better with a few horses' heads looking out," said David Peterborough.

A tall man of about sixty with grey hair appeared from the saddle-room and David Peterborough said: "Hallo, Small, our guests have arrived."

The Days and Laurence and I all said: "Good afternoon," at the same moment.

Mr. Small said: "It is one too. It'll be hot tomorrow down on that course, with no shelter within five miles." All the time he was speaking Mr. Small had been looking our horses over. Now he said: "Aren't there too many of you? I can count six horses."

I felt embarrassed. I looked at Valentine, at Andrew, at Kate, but none of them said anything.

"Yes," I said, "I'm awfully sorry. I counted wrong. I never realised that Harry was coming with us."

"That's quite all right," said David Peterborough. "The more the merrier. There's lots of room."

Mr. Small yelled: "Dick," and when a boy of about sixteen appeared he said: "Get Sportsman's box ready."

"Can't we help?" asked Andrew. We had all dismounted.

"Yes," said Kate. "I'll fetch some straw."

"Dick will do it," said Mr. Small, removing our saddles with amazing rapidity. "He knows his way about better than what you would."

Mr. Small directed us and we put our horses into boxes, assisted by David Peterborough and Dick. The boxes were bedded deep in wheat straw and in each corner there hung a hay net filled with mixture hay. In another corner there were teak buckets, initialled D.P., and filled with water.

"I'll give them each a feed presently," said Mr. Small.

"They're lovely boxes," said Kate.

"Now run along in and have some tea," said Mr. Small. "Dick and I can manage now."

"But can't we rub them down or anything?" asked Kate.

"Mummy's bringing the night rugs when she comes

to fetch us," I said.

"What about the tack?" asked Laurence. "Can we clean it after tea? Or shall we take it back with us?"

"We'll see to that," said Mr. Small.

"Come on," said David Peterborough. "Tea's waiting."

Inside, the house smelt of furniture polish. We were greeted by two West Highland terriers and a collie. "Morag, Hamish and Solomon," said David Peterborough, introducing them. "All very Scottish."

David Peterborough left us to wash our hands and Kate said: "I think he's jolly nice," and Harry said: "It's not at all as I expected. I thought the house would be dark and full of antlers. And he doesn't seem to mind my turning up out of the blue, at all," he added in surprised accents.

In the drawing-room we found a woman wearing slacks, lying on the floor and playing with the dogs. Her hair was all on end and if it hadn't been grey, I should have said her age was between twenty and thirty.

"Hallo, you've arrived," she said, jumping to her feet when she saw us.

I said: "Yes, that's right, an awful avalanche I'm afraid." Kate said: "I love your dogs," and Valentine said: "I'm afraid we're rather late."

Then we heard a bell ringing and the woman said: "That means tea."

David appeared with a Swiss goat bell in his hand and said: "Tea is served," in a silly, refined voice with a giggle in it.

Kate and I began to laugh.

David Peterborough said: "Of course, I haven't introduced you. To tell the truth, I really only know Sandy. Anyway, this is my mother."

Kate gave a loud gasp and I said: "How do you do?" very loudly to hide it.

When we had all shaken hands and I had explained exactly which of us was which, we wandered into the dining-room for tea. Lady Peterborough was very amusing. We all laughed a great deal during tea and ate large hunks of sticky lardy cake.

Lady Peterborough, we discovered, knew Mummy's sister Sarah quite well, and we discussed our aunt's peculiarities for some time.

Then David Peterborough said: "And how's the hunt?" and for a moment a dreadful silence fell.

Then Laurence said: "Oh, fine thanks," in a voice which sounded a little too bright, and Valentine said: "We made a lot out of the ball," in an obvious effort to change the subject.

"How are the puppies?" asked David Peterborough. "I suppose you've got some again this year?"

"Yes," said Kate. "Nine couple. Rosa, Rory, Romeo, Romper, Roma, Tyrant, Torchlight, Tawny, Tapestry, Raider, Raftsman, Random, Rajah, Rhapsody, Ravenous, Rouser, Ravager and Rhonda."

"What heavenly names," said Lady Peterborough.

"Can we come round and see them when we come back from the South of France?" asked David Peterborough. "I should like to walk a couple for you, if you think I'm a suitable person."

"Oh, that would be marvellous," I cried.

The Days were looking at one another and saying

nothing. I wondered whether David Peterborough had forgotten our conversation in the tea-shop.

The next moment Kate upset her cup of tea. "Oh, I'm sorry," she cried. "I don't know why I'm so clumsy."

"That's quite all right," said David Peterborough, springing to his feet. "It doesn't matter a bit."

He rushed from the room, and returning with a clean tea-towel, he mopped the table rather ineffectively and then threw the towel behind the door.

Laurence looked at me and muttered: "Mummy will be here in about five minutes. It's getting dreadfully late."

Lady Peterborough poured tea into saucers for the dogs. By the time Mummy arrived we all felt that we had known the Peterboroughs for years. We wandered out together and I introduced Mummy, and we took the rugs round to the stables and rugged up our horses, who looked very content. Then we said good-bye to David Peterborough and his mother and David said: "Remember, there's no need for you to be here much before nine tomorrow. The show ground is only three miles away."

And Lady Peterborough said: "I hope you win everything, and put those horrid Symington women in their place."

I said: "Not likely, I'm afraid," and Andrew said: "We'll do our best, and please remember you're welcome to come round the kennels any time before June," which caused David Peterborough to give me a look which told me all too plainly that he had by no means forgotten the conversation between us in The Country Kitchen.

"We'll be back by the twenty-ninth. Will the thirtieth be too late?" asked David Peterborough.

"No, of course not," replied Laurence rather quickly, obviously anxious to get a word in before Andrew. "Any time you like will be all right."

"But it will be best to ring up first," said Andrew, "just in case we're all out."

"Okay," said David Peterborough.

Mummy had started the car. We said good-bye again, and thank you. Then waving madly out of all the car windows at once we left The Limes.

"They seem nice," commented Mummy as we reached the road.

"They are," said Laurence.

"Frightfully," said Kate.

"We had a super tea," cried Harry. "And there's a groom called Small, who's enormous."

"Wasn't Lady Peterborough young?" said Kate. "I thought she must be his wife at first."

"Same here," said Valentine.

"I told you she needn't be more than fifty," said Andrew.

"I imagined her fearfully old," I said. "With an ebony cane and lace and a shawl."

"Wasn't it embarrassing when he said he'd walk a puppy for us?" said Valentine.

"Dreadful," said Kate.

"I can't see why," said Laurence, in an unusually aggressive voice.

"*Red night, shepherd's delight,*" I quoted, gazing out of the window across green fields, to where the woods of home were blue in the distance.

"There'll be a mist in the morning," said Andrew. "I

wish we could have hunted longer. I should like to hunt in May. Packs do, you know."

"Yes, I know," replied Laurence. "The packs in Cumberland and Westmorland, the Lakeland packs, the mountain packs."

It was rather a squash in the car. Kate and I were in the front together with Mummy. The others were in the back.

"I suppose we'll have to wear our black coats tomorrow, however hot it is," said Kate.

"Yes, definitely," replied Laurence. "We can't possibly jump round hunter trials in shirt sleeves. It just isn't done."

We dropped the Days at Long Chill Farm. When they had gone I felt as though a weight had been lifted from my mind. We drove down the lane, and when we were out of earshot, Laurence cried, in a voice sharp with irritation, "Oh, Andrew does infuriate me. Why must he be so defeatist?"

"Because he's in despair," I said.

"I know it's beastly for them," Laurence answered. "But I can't see why he must be so deliberately difficult. Look at that silly advertisement he showed us to-day. Why should he start advertising hounds now when the sale's not till August? Anyway, they belong to us, too."

"Perhaps Mr. Day is being difficult," suggested Mummy.

"I hadn't thought of that," said Laurence. "It's all so horrid; particularly as I'm quite certain that somehow everything's going to turn out all right."

"I don't see how," I said. "But I feel just the same.

And I'm simply terrified that the Days will give up too soon."

"Before the miracle happens," said Laurence. "I know, it's an awful feeling."

"You're both terrible Mr. Micawbers, like all the Darlingtons," said Mummy as we reached Little Hall.

TEN

Mummy and Daddy agreed to take Mr. and Mrs. Day to the hunter trials in our car, so that the rest of us could go to The Limes together in the landrover.

There was a mist, as Andrew had predicted, when Laurence and I rose from our beds at seven. We ate a hasty breakfast together in the kitchen, feeling rather lost without any horses to feed or boxes to muck out. We took our parents cups of tea and made toast and coffee for their breakfast. Then we set off together, on our feet, across the valley.

The mist was already lifting. We felt hot in our black coats and walking in boots made our legs ache.

We found the Days waiting for us by the landrover, which was parked in front of the farmhouse.

"Bert Saunders offered to feed hounds for us," said Andrew, when we were within earshot. "So we haven't had to rush at all."

"How very nice of him," said Laurence. "I suppose we'd better make the day after tomorrow's pudding tonight."

"Yes, when we get back," replied Andrew. "I hope

we're not too late. The meat's all ready, so it shouldn't take long."

We climbed into the landrover and Kate said: "I hope the horses have slept all right. I do wish David Peterborough hadn't said we weren't to be there till nine. It seems dreadfully late."

"Especially when we've got to plait," said Valentine.

Andrew started the landrover. "It won't take us long to get there," he said.

"Thirty minutes I should think," said Laurence.

"Less than that," replied Andrew, driving very fast down the lane.

He drove even faster when we reached the road. We tore through Allate at between forty and fifty miles an hour, and at every corner he hooted furiously.

"We'll be there by half-past eight with any luck," he said, passing a brand new Jaguar. The landrover speedometer hovered round seventy.

"Pass that one, pass that one," shrieked Harry, seeing a Fiesta.

"Don't be silly," said Valentine. "We won't get there at all if we crash. You might be sensible, Andrew."

"Thirty mile limit ahead," shrieked Harry.

Andrew drove more cautiously through Childlington, which was fortunate because we passed several policemen. But he increased his speed again when we had left the town behind.

Laurence made a face at me which meant, what's the matter with Andrew this morning? I remembered the way he had ridden after the children's meet. He had been stupidly reckless then. Obviously, he was in the same mood today.

"Steady Andrew," said Valentine, as we swept past a large Bentley travelling at fifty miles an hour or more.

The day is too lovely for a crash, I thought, looking at the rich farmland on each side of us. Hooting loudly, we swept past a lorry loaded with sacks. I glanced at my companions and saw that Andrew looked grim. Kate, who was in the back, was clutching the front seat with both hands. Harry appeared the happiest. He was enjoying himself. "Faster, faster," he cried at intervals, and "pass it, pass it," when he saw a car in front. Laurence was being a back seat driver: his hands were following each movement of the steering wheel; his feet trod imaginary pedals.

At last, we saw The Limes ahead. Valentine sighed with relief and Kate relaxed her hold on the front seat.

"Just made it," said Andrew, with satisfaction in his voice, as he swung up the drive and we could all see that the hands of the stable clock were at half-past eight.

We parked and found Mr. Small and Dick mucking out the last of the boxes.

"You're early," Mr. Small called when he saw us.

Our horses had been fed and their boxes were clean.

"Oh, aren't we lucky?" said Kate, as we fetched grooming tools from the landrover.

We took off our coats and rolled up our sleeves and, wishing to impress Mr. Small and Dick, we groomed with far more energy than usual. Presently Mr. Small came and watched me over my box door.

"The Governor's gone to town," he said. "Left first thing this morning."

"Isn't he going to the hunter trials then?" I asked,

surprised and rather disappointed.

"Well, he was yesterday, but it doesn't look much like it today," answered Mr. Small. "I don't know what's come over him. I expect it's leaving tomorrow and all. Probably he's forgotten to buy the tickets, or something like that. You never know."

Being watched by Mr. Small gave me the jitters. First, I dropped my body-brush, then I lost the curry-comb. Luckily, Daystar was unusually clean, so I didn't have to wash her. But beneath the gaze of Mr. Small's expert eye, I fumbled with her tail bandage, putting it on first with a twist in it and then, after having taken it off again, rolling it up with the tapes outside instead of inside. After a few minutes, Mr. Small could bear to witness my clumsy efforts no longer.

"That's no way to put on a tail bandage," he said, and opening the box door, "Here, let me do it."

A moment later Laurence appeared.

"Oh, Sandy," he said, "I can't get Overture's first plait right. I wish you'd come and look. It's really awful, all straggly and horribly loose. It looks like a first effort by a child of six."

I looked at Mr. Small, who had picked up my body-brush and curry-comb.

"You go on," he said. "I'll finish your mare."

Overture's first plait really did look rather awful. It was fat and loose and already beginning to come undone.

"Can you improve it? Or are you going to scrap it altogether?" asked Laurence, watching me anxiously.

"Scrap it," I answered, cutting out Laurence's sewing efforts.

"My fingers all seem thumbs this morning," said Laurence, sounding more cheerful. "Look, I'll thread the needle for you; just pass it along each time you're ready," which meant, I realised that Laurence expected me to plait Overture's entire mane.

"I don't know how many I can do," I said, parting the mane into seven even portions. "I've still got Daystar's to do."

Laurence made no answer. Farther down the yard, the Days were shouting remarks to one another. I plaited furiously. When I had done half Overture's mane, Laurence left the box and took a peep at Daystar. He returned jubilant.

"Mr. Small's plaiting her mane," he told me. "He's doing it beautifully."

"Oh, good," I said, feeling pleased.

"Dick's helping the Days," Laurence said.

At last I finished Overture's mane. "Seven plaits and a forelock," said Laurence. "Thanks awfully. You have done her beautifully."

"I bet they're not such good plaits as Daystar's," I said. "And Overture's mane's easier to do, so really, I've scored."

"We're putting on our saddles," cried Kate, peering into the box. "It's nearly half-past nine."

Laurence and I collected our tack from the saddle-room. It had been beautifully cleaned. Every buckle glinted in the sunlight and we could see our faces in the stirrups.

Harry appeared with a tin of hoof oil and a brush and oiled our horses' hoofs.

"Dick's jolly nice," he told us. "He's groomed

Lollipop for ages. He's got three brothers and one of them's a speedway rider."

We loaded our rugs and grooming tools into the landrover, which Andrew was to drive to the show ground while the rest of us rode there leading Mulligatawny.

Andrew said: "I'll thank Mr. Small and Dick formally," and Laurence said: "Okay."

"Gosh, I'm excited," cried Kate, as she led Dusty out into the sunshine and mounted. "I'm really determined to do well today."

We all thanked Mr. Small and Dick at some length before riding away from the yard, past Sportsman and the other hunters in the paddock, down the drive and out into the sunlit road.

"Dick's told me the way," said Valentine, turning left. "It's quite simple—straight nearly all the way."

"Oh, I am excited," cried Kate again.

"So am I!" shrieked Harry.

I felt too excited to speak. I wanted us to jump clear rounds more than I could say. I didn't mind much whether we won the classes or not. I only wanted us to redeem the reputation of the Chill Valley Hunt servants for all time.

"I wonder if those two horrid women will be there?" cried Kate. "Won't it be fun if we beat them?"

Laurence and I had entered our horses in two showing classes as well as in the hunter trial events. Overture was in a class for hunters, and I had entered Daystar, who is fourteen hands three, in a class for hacks. We had both entered for the Novice jumping, which Andrew and Valentine were in for too. In the hunter trial events, we had all, except Kate and Harry, entered for the Open Class. Kate and I were together in the pairs again and so were Valentine and Andrew. Kate had also entered for the pony class and for the hunter trial event for people of sixteen years and under. Harry was in the smallest showing and jumping classes.

We discussed our entries as we followed the unfamiliar road through the open, almost treeless, countryside. The Novice class was for unaffiliated horses.

"I don't suppose I shall be anywhere in the showing class," said Kate, patting Dusty. "I've never been in anything like that before."

"I hope we don't have to do a lot of fancy stuff in the hack class," said Valentine. "I haven't practised changing legs at all."

"You won't need to do a flying change; an ordinary one will do," said Laurence.

"I wish I had entered for the hunter class instead," said Valentine. "Golden Syrup's got a jolly good gallop."

"I hope Lollipop doesn't nap," said Harry. "What will happen if he gallops me out of the ring?"

"I should think you'd be disqualified," answered Laurence.

We reached the show ground and saw the ring surrounded by a white rail and, beyond it, the hunter trial course stretching across open downland country.

"But half of it's made up," cried Kate, looking at an in and out built out of rails in an open field. Farther on there was a black brush with huge wings and a guard rail in front.

"It looks a terrifying course," said Valentine.

"Look at that one," said Laurence, pointing to another

brush fence, this time with an open ditch in front.

"Gosh, it looks enormous," cried Kate.

"We'll be clever if we jump clear rounds today," said Laurence. Andrew passed us, hooting loudly.

My tummy seemed to be sinking inside me. I couldn't imagine any of us jumping a clear round over such a formidable course. There were dozens of horse boxes parked in rows a little way from the ring.

A class of shire horses was being judged as we entered the show ground.

"Oh, dear, I feel quite sick. It really is an enormous show," said Kate.

I felt awful. There seemed no hope now of us doing anything to improve the reputation of ourselves or the hunt. We'd all refuse three times on the hunter trial course, I thought, and ride home in indescribable gloom; and it would be all my fault.

"I don't think it's a particularly large show," said Laurence, his tone belying his words.

Daystar felt excited. She jogged and cantered instead of walking.

"She does look lovely," said Kate. "I'm sure she'll be somewhere in the showing."

"Not likely," I said, wishing that I could compliment Dusty in the same way. He is nice looking, with a good head and a large eye, but no show pony.

"I've got all our numbers," said Andrew, appearing. "And here's a programme. There are fifty-four entries in the Novice jumping. The next class is for hunters, so you'd better look slippy, Laurence."

We tied on Laurence's number, and Andrew polished Overture with a rubber and Harry oiled her hoofs again and Valentine brushed her tail, and the microphone called all competitors for Class Three into the collecting ring.

"That's you," said Andrew. "Good luck."

"Good luck," the rest of us echoed, as Laurence rode away across the show ground.

"I hope he wins something," said Kate.

"Same here," said Valentine.

Laurence rode into the ring, third. He looked odd among the other competitors. He sat farther forward in his saddle, and his shoulders were square. His legs were farther back, too, and his reins were shorter.

"He does look peculiar," said Kate.

Overture looked odd too. She was considerably smaller than the other horses, and lacked substance when compared with them. Her shoulder looked straight and her tail seemed set-on too low down. Laurence had made the mistake of carrying a hunting whip. His fellow competitors all had leather-covered canes.

The hunters walked round the ring for ages, while the judges pointed first at one and then another.

"Oh, I do think judging's dull," cried Kate when five minutes had elapsed. "Why don't they get on and do something?"

"If you watched you might learn something," said Valentine smugly.

A steward shouted "Trot," and the hunters increased their pace.

"If you're going to horse deal you'll need an eye for a horse, Kate," said Valentine. "I place the grey lying second, first. What do the rest of you think?"

"I wonder what he's like across country," mused

Andrew. "This isn't really much of a test for a hunter. They all look so large to me. I wouldn't want to gallop any of them, except Overture, through some of our woods."

"I shouldn't want to whip-in on them either," said Kate.

"Don't you think we're being rather unsporting?" asked Valentine.

"It's not a working hunter class." "Everyone's entitled to their own opinion," replied Andrew.

"The hunters were galloping. They looked beautiful in the sunlight. They made me think of hunting. "Someone should blow the gone away," I said.

"They certainly can move," said Valentine, watching them thunder by. Overture looked very excited. She was trying to cut the corners and pass the horses in front. Laurence's hat had slipped over one eye. He looked harrassed and unhappy when compared with the other competitors in the ring, who all looked calm, cool and collected, or else faintly bored.

"Walk," cried the steward, and the big hunters came back to hand, a few of them after frantic boring efforts with their heads between their knees, but most of them quite calmly as though they had been waiting for that very moment. Overture, alone, misbehaved. She cantered sideways and looking towards us, neighed loudly. "How unsophisticated," said Valentine.

The judges started to call in the front line. They put the grey we had liked top and, when they collected eight or nine horses, they told the rest of the competitors to make a back line.

"Well, that's that," cried Andrew.

"What a swindle," cried Harry. "I think Overture looks much the nicest."

"Ssh," said Valentine. "Don't shriek so."

"I call it a beastly waste of money," cried Kate. "At least in hunter trials you get the fun of riding round the course."

"I'm not looking forward to the hack class much," I said, wondering whether I would look as peculiar as Laurence in the ring.

"Why on earth don't they let Laurence come out?" asked Kate. "They obviously don't want him any more."

"Do stop critising," cried Valentine. "You're just as bad as those two women in hairnets."

The judges were riding the hunters now. Andrew looked at the programme.

"That's the Master of the Littleton," he said, pointing to the judge riding the grey. "He came out once with the Path Hill. I thought I recognised him. They both seem to be M.F.H.'s; the other one is the Master of the . . . goodness, the East Nightley."

"Gosh!" cried Kate.

"We ought to have recognised him," cried Harry. "After all we did hunt with his hounds one day."

At that moment the microphone called all competitors for the hack class into the collecting ring, and Valentine and I, having never shown a horse before in our lives, both panicked.

"Quick, take off my tail bandage, somebody," cried Valentine.

"Where's the hoof oil?" I shrieked, looking frantically at everyone but Harry, who actually had it in his hand.

"You've got lots of time," said Kate.

"Don't panic," said Andrew. I mounted, forgetting to tighten my girths and the saddle slipped round.

"More haste, less speed," chanted Harry.

"Don't be beastly," said Kate, coming to my rescue.

The hunters were being led in hand without their saddles. I saw that my parents and Mr. and Mrs. Day had arrived. I mounted again, and Valentine said: "I haven't a stick. I must have a cane or something. Supposing Golden Syrup naps."

"Here, have this," said Kate, offering her hunting whip.

"No, *thank* you," said Valentine. "That won't do at all. I'd rather have nothing than a hunting whip."

"Try borrowing from someone when you reach the collecting ring," advised Andrew.

"But they'll all want theirs," answered Valentine.

"Well, I don't know what you're to do then," said Andrew.

Valentine and I rode to the collecting ring together in gloomy silence. We felt out of place among the other competitors in our class. Their horses were far better turned out than our own; their tails were elegantly pulled, their manes were thin and beautifully plaited; their skin seemed to ripple as they moved, and their coats shone in the sunshine. I felt peculiar in my black hunting coat, from which I had removed the scarlet facings for the occasion. My legs felt in the wrong place, and like Laurence, I seemed to be sitting too far forward in the saddle. The other competitors rode their hacks round and round the collecting ring, while we waited for the hunter class to end. Valentine and I stood together whispering remarks to one another about them. At last, the hunters came out.

"This is just a waste of time," said Valentine, as we entered the ring.

"Good luck," called Laurence as he passed.

"We'll need it," I said, feeling happier now that the worst was happening.

A tall, thin man in a bowler hat and with beautifully polished brown boots, and a woman in a dark blue coat, breeches, bowler hat and boots, had taken the place of the two M.F.H.s. Daystar felf fresh and sensible at the same time, and I could feel that she was going well. We walked and trotted and then a steward shouted: "Canter," and several people rode past me on the inside. Valentine was in difficulties, because Golden Syrup couldn't canter as slowly as the other horses. Several times she found herself within five yards of someone's hindquarters and received withering glances from the competitor on top. I noticed that Mummy and Daddy were sitting in an enclosure, and then suddenly I realised that the steward was shouting: "Twenty-five, come in please," and beckoning frantically at me.

For a few wonderful moments I thought that I was standing first. I rode in, and feeling very self-conscious, stood in the centre of the ring. I patted Daystar and thought, perhaps we haven't been so silly after all, and imagined another red rosette hanging in the saddle room at home. Then I noticed Valentine coming towards me and another girl on a very ancient grey, and my wonderful illusion was shattered, for I knew then that we were forming the back line, not the front, and that our horses were actually the worst hacks in the class. I patted Daystar and whispered that I'd rather ride her than all the most beautiful hacks in the world.

"They soon sorted us out," said Valentine with a smile.

"I'm always in the back line," said the girl on the ancient grey. "I've never been anywhere else. I don't know why I go on showing, really. I suppose it's crazy. But I just can't stop."

"I don't think it'll get me that way," I said, thinking that I never wanted to ride in another hack class.

"Nor me," said Valentine. "Though I'd like to show hunters side-saddle."

More people were joining us in the back line every moment now. They were all very cheerful, in fact most of them seemed to have expected such a fate. It was very hot in the centre of the ring. Daystar was sweating and, looking at my fellow competitors, I realised that I should be wearing gloves.

The judges began to call in the front line. The few competitors left in the ring had their ears and eyes fixed firmly on the judges. A nod was enough to bring them walking into the centre, still looking completely unperturbed. When there were no horses left walking round, one of the judges turned to the back line and said: "You may leave the ring now if you like," and we all trotted out together, feeling rather like children who had just been let out of class.

"Thank goodness that's over," said Valentine, as we cantered towards the Days and Laurence.

"Bad luck," said Kate.

"They're all pals, that's what it is," said Mr. Day, and we all cried out in horror to hear such a remark, so reminiscent of the two women in hairnets, on the lips of Mr. Day. "What's the matter?" he demanded. "It's true, isn't it?"

"No, it is *not*," said Valentine. "Golden Syrup may be a good performer, but she's *not* a hack, and never will be."

Valentine and Mr. Day were glaring at each other angrily. I hoped there wasn't going to be a family row.

"They didn't seem to think much of you," called Daddy, approaching.

"And Daystar looked so nice," said Mummy.

"And nearly all the competitors stick their legs too far forward," cried Kate. "Just look at them. I thought I rode badly, but compared with theirs, my leg position is wonderful. And their reins!"

"They're calling you, Kate," said Valentine, as the microphone asked all competitors for class four to go into the collecting ring, please.

At the same moment Laurence cried: "Look," and pointed to the hunter trial course, round which someone was already riding. "They've started," he cried. "Come on, we're in the first class."

We all deserted Kate. We mounted hurriedly and galloped to the other collecting ring at the other end of the show ground. I reached it first.

"We never knew you had begun," I gasped at the steward in charge. "We're in this class."

Already, I saw our entrance money wasted, and us never jumping the course which had looked so terrifying earlier, but which, now I might never have a chance to ride it, looked easy and ideal for Daystar.

"That's all right," said the steward, smiling. "There's still lots of time. There's thirty entries in the class, and that's only the second one going round. Can I have your numbers?"

Laurence sighed with relief.

"Twenty-five, twenty-six, twenty-seven, and twenty-eight," said Valentine.

"You'll be wanted in about another twenty to thirty minutes," said the steward, consulting a list.

We rode back to the other ring feeling rather stupid. Two women in felt hats were judging the ponies. Kate was cantering round the ring looking incredibly happy. But Dusty looked quite unlike the other ponies, which were lighter in build, with better fronts and longer strides.

"Let's go and have some elevenses," suggested Laurence, sounding disheartened.

At the far end of the ring a band was playing. We held our horses while we drank tea out of thermos flasks, and ate biscuits.

Presently, Kate joined us. "It wasn't nearly as bad as I expected," she said, patting Dusty. "Some of the other competitors were awfully nice, and one of the judges wanted to know whether I had ridden a lot and the other one asked Dusty's age."

"What did you say?" asked Valentine.

"That Dusty was only fifteen and that she was a hunt horse, and that I had ridden since I was six," replied Kate.

Harry was entering the ring on Lollipop. He had watched the other classes with rapt attention, now he was riding with long reins and his legs stuck forward.

"He'll fall off if he does that when they canter," said Valentine.

"What did they say when you appeared in the other collecting ring?" asked Kate.

"That the class had only just started and that they didn't want us for twenty minutes or so," said Laurence.

"What did I say?" cried Valentine, as the ponies in the ring started to canter. "Harry will never manage Lollipop riding like that."

We could all see that Lollipop's attention was riveted to the collecting ring. Harry's reins were becoming longer and longer.

"If he brings him out this time, he will in the jumping, too," said Valentine.

"And Dad will be so cross," said Kate.

"It's obvious he's going to," said Andrew, as Lollipop put on a spurt and passed the two ponies in front of him.

"What a disgrace," moaned Kate.

Harry had lost a stirrup. He was leaning too far forward and his hands were on Lollipop's withers.

"I don't believe he wants to stop," said Andrew.

"If only he would shorten his reins!" cried Valentine.

Harry had become a mere passenger. Lollipop gave a triumphant buck as he neared the collecting ring.

"Oh, he is naughty," cried Kate.

"You ought to school him," said Valentine. "You're lighter than I am."

"There isn't much time left for that," said Andrew.

Valentine made a rude face at Andrew.

Lollipop neighed raucously, and with another buck, he dashed through the collecting ring, barged past the steward who tried to stop him, and with Harry still crouching on his neck, galloped full speed across the show ground, only stopping when he reached us.

"Oh, isn't he naughty?" gasped Harry when he stopped, regaining his stirrups and kicking wildly.

"I'll go back with you," said Kate, mounting Dusty.

"You should have shortened your reins," said Valentine severely.

Kate and Harry rode away together, but when they reached the collecting ring, the steward there said: "They don't want you any more, son," so they came back again with broad grins on their faces.

"Lollipop got sick of it," Harry told us, "and I don't blame him. I think showing's jolly dull."

"That wasn't much of a performance, was it?" Mr. Day grumbled.

"I think we'd better go across to the hunter trial course now," said Andrew. "I'm sure twenty minutes must have passed."

"Let's hope we do better there," said Valentine.

ELEVEN

The hunter trial collecting ring steward greeted us cheerfully.

"I shan't keep you long now," he said with a smile.

"Oh, dear, now I feel sick again," said Kate. "I do hope you do well. The course looks bigger every moment."

"Nonsense, it's quite small," said Andrew.

"But the ditch!" cried Kate. "I'm sure I shall fall in it and get all wet."

"There's no water in it," said the steward.

"Oh, good!" cried Kate. "That's a relief."

"Our horses should be all right over water, anyway," said Andrew. "They've jumped enough streams in their lives."

"Look," shrieked Kate. "There are those two dreadful women again. Hurray! I did so want them to come. We must do well now."

"Ssh," said Valentine. "Do try to behave sensibly."

"They do look awful," said Harry. "Just like two disagreeable school teachers."

"You're next but one," the steward told Laurence.

"But I haven't learnt the course yet," cried Laurence in a voice filled with despair.

"We ought to have walked it. Why didn't we?" demanded Andrew. "We are lunatics."

The steward started to explain the course to Laurence. I listened frantically. There seemed to be a multitude of flags we must keep outside.

"I know I shall never learn it," cried Kate. "It sounds terribly difficult."

"Ssh, do be quiet," said Valentine.

"Did you say the brush with the ditch was before the stiles?" asked Laurence.

"The jumps do look big," cried Harry. "Do you think you'll get round, Laurence?"

"Ssh," said Valentine. "Do be quiet."

"Okay, I think I've got it," said Laurence in rather an uncertain voice.

"Let's run through it again," said the steward, which we all thought was very kind of him.

"First the brush with the rail in front, next the rails." he said, pointing. "Then the in and out, a left turn round the flag, and over the open ditch and brush, then over the stile; another turn, this time to the right, and over the gates, then left again and over the brush you can just see with the rail on the landing side, the one on the slope of the hill; next over the rails at the top and right round a flag you can't see from here; over a double oxer; and then over the long low hedge you can just see from here and past the winning post."

"It's a dreadfully long course," said Kate.

"Eleven fences and mile and a quarter across country," said the steward. "I helped to build it, so I know."

The starter was waving his shooting stick in our direction and making frantic faces.

"Your turn," the steward told Laurence. "Number twenty-six," he shouted.

"Good luck," we all said.

"Do you think Overture can do it?" asked Mummy, suddenly beside me. "It does look rather a big course."

"Oh, yes, I'm sure she can," I said, though in my heart of hearts, I doubted it, and doubted that Daystar and I could, still more. Laurence started.

"Oh, I *do* hope he does well," cried Kate.

Someone behind us said: "That's the Master of the Chill Valley Hunt. He should make a good round."

I turned in my saddle, but I couldn't see who had spoken. Laurence had reached the first brush with the rail in front. Overture lengthened her stride and jumped it magnificently with inches to spare. My hopes soared.

"She does jump beautifully now," said Valentine.

"That looked all right," said Daddy, who had joined us. Overture took the rails in the same effortless style. The two disagreeable women in hairnets had arrived and were standing just behind us.

"That's one of those mad Chill Valley children," said the tallest, quite as though she approved of us. I wanted to cry: "But they can't have practiced over the course this time," as Overture jumped the in and out perfectly and galloped on towards the open ditch.

"Steady, steady, not too fast," cried Andrew, as Laurence pushed Overture on.

I could hardly bear to look. If only he clears it, I thought, and then Overture took off feet in front and landed far out on the other side.

"Gosh!" cried Kate.

"That mare's good enough for Badminton," said a man behind us.

"Yes, I know," I said, imagining Laurence winning there against the best horsemen in the world.

"What's his number?" someone asked their companion.

"He seems to be doing all right," said Daddy in a satisfied voice.

The rest of the course seemed nothing to Overture. She cleared every fence with plenty to spare.

There was a burst of clapping as she passed the finishing post, and Kate cried: "Gosh, that was a marvellous round."

I saw that another competitor had started and that the starter was waving frantically at me.

"Go on," said the steward. "If you do as well as your brother you'll be all right. Number twenty-five," he shouted.

"Good luck," said Kate.

"Keep calm," advised Valentine.

"I'm sure I don't know the course," I cried, with a feeling of hopelessness, thinking: Brush rails . . . what then? I shall lose my way, I know I shall.

"Of course you know it, Sandy," said Andrew in reassuring tones. "It's quite straightforward, anyway. Just follow the flags."

"It's easy to say that, I thought. But it's not straight and I don't know it.

"The jumps are numbered," shouted the steward.

"Good luck," shouted Mummy.

The starter patted Daystar. "Are you ready?" he asked. I nodded. "Off," he cried. I forgot everything then but the course in front of me. The first brush looked very black and very large. It sloped away from me and the rail in front was thick and strong. Daystar felt wonderful; fit and calm and capable of galloping for hours. She lengthened her stride as we neared the brush. I let her choose her own pace, and we were over with plenty to spare. I felt more confident then. She took the rails in the same style and cleared the in and out with the greatest of ease. Now the open ditch, I thought, pushing Daystar on a little with my legs. It looked very wide, and quite bottomless, though it can't have been. Daystar hesitated for one split second, then she increased her pace and the ditch was beneath us and then we were over. I patted her and thought, now for the hill, and turned right. Daystar's wonderful, I decided—leaning well forward as we reached the hill. She wasn't blowing at all. I must keep calm, I thought. There were cries as I neared the brush fence. I looked ahead and saw that the approach was clear. Perhaps they're calling their dogs, I thought, sending Daystar on with my legs. The brush didn't frighten me at all, now that I had jumped the one with the ditch in front. I saw the guard rail on the other side when we were in mid air, the next second we were over and it was then that the meaning of the shouts penetrated my brain.

Two stewards were shouting: "Stop, stop," and waving flags. I felt an awful sinking feeling in the pit of my stomach. I changed Daystar's gallop to a trot and then to a walk. What have I done? I wondered.

"You've gone wrong," shouted one of the men running towards me. "You should have gone over the stile after the ditch and then over the gate, before turning.

I am a fool, I thought, feeling horribly sick. Daystar was jumping so beautifully, why did I have to spoil it all?

The judges were waving from the top of the hill.

"You'd better get off the course," the steward told me. "There's another horse coming."

I patted Daystar and thanked the steward several times, which must have sounded rather silly. Then I saw that the rider approaching was Andrew and I hurried away from the brush fence.

Mulligatawny was blowing a good deal. He took off rather too near the brush and rapped the rail on the landing side. The steward waved his flag in the direction of the judges. I rode back round the fences towards the collecting ring with a heavy heart. I could only think, I am a fool, I am a fool, I am a fool, over and over again. I felt hot and red in the face, and weary. I wanted to hide from the Days but they had already seen me.

"Bad luck," shouted Kate, when I was within earshot.

"Wasn't I an idiot?" I yelled back.

"Everybody does it sometime in their lives," said Andrew calmly, appearing with a sweating Mulligatawny. "It's a dickens of a course, though." I patted Daystar again. "She jumped marvellously," said Andrew.

"Now what did you want to do that for?" asked Mr. Day when he saw me. "You were doing such a good round, too."

"Bad luck," said a woman I had never seen before,

astride a dark-brown horse. "I did that last week at the Littleton trials. Makes you feel awful, doesn't it?"

"Awful," I agreed, beginning to feel slightly less dismal.

"People here seem much nicer than the ones at our hunter trials," Kate whispered to me. "They've been saying all sorts of nice things about us."

"Apparently, judging by their comments," said Laurence, who had been listening, "we've got a simply wonderful reputation. Our hounds possess terrific drive; we're marvellous; our horses are absolutely first class; and no one can stay near any of us when we run."

"Unfortunately, it's all come too late," said Andrew in a dismal voice. "Things like that always happen when you've got to give up."

Laurence made a face at me which meant, isn't he too pessimistic for words?

Andrew said: "Did you happen to look at *Horse and Hound* this morning?"

"No, we left too early," said Laurence. "It hadn't come."

"Well, there's an advertisement for our horses in it. Dad sent it in. Kate doesn't know yet, so don't shout about it," Andrew said.

I looked at Laurence and read despair in his face. Suddenly it seemed as though the end had come. The end of our pack, and the end of the Days, as far as the hunt was concerned. I knew now why Andrew had driven so recklessly in the morning; why he had been unusually silent all day; so calm about everything as though nothing really mattered any more. There seemed nothing left to say, and absolutely nothing that Laurence or I could do to save the situation.

The microphone announced Number Twenty-Six as

the winner of the open hunter trial class and it was some moments before we realised that Laurence's number was twenty-six and that he and Overture were first. Andrew and I were horribly calm about it. We only said, "Jolly good," in dismal voices, and Laurence rode to receive his rosette with a grim expression on his face.

I thought of people who believe that fame is only dust and ashes when you get it, that *it is better to travel hopefully than to arrive*, and it seemed to me then that their philosophy was true. It was horrid to realise that we had now almost all the things we had ever wanted—a marvellous entry of our own young hounds, a wonderful reputation, a satisfactory bank balance, and dozens of friendly farmers—and yet soon we would lose them all.

"Isn't it wonderful?" said Mummy. "I'm so pleased. Overture did go beautifully."

"Yes, beautifully," I agreed, with my mind far away.

It's all over now, I thought, there's no point in hoping any more.

"Sandy, it's lunch time," said Laurence, some time later, waking me from my reverie.

We all walked to the landrover in the gloomiest silence imaginable. Apparently, Kate had heard about the advertisement, and she sniffed endlessly, except when she stopped to blow her nose into a large red-spotted handkerchief.

"Do you know we've missed the novice jumping?" asked Valentine. "Apparently it was after the pony class."

"I don't suppose we'd have done much anyway," said Andrew.

"Probably refused three times," I said glumly.

hought the horses were yours," said Laurence, ng to Andrew. "I mean that you each owned your o r."

"They were and they weren't, Andrew answered. "Dad bought them in the beginning, and he more or less gave them to us; but not with any ceremony or anything like that, so in a way they're still his."

"Anyway, if the farm's going we can't very well keep them," said Kate with a sniff.

We watered and fed the horses and tied them to a rail apparently erected for that purpose. We unpacked the picnic baskets but none of us felt much like lunch.

Laurence ate a sandwich, the Days each ate a biscuit and I ate nothing. Then we put everything back in the baskets and returned them to the landrover. After that, we lay on our backs in the sunshine. I shall ask Mummy whether I can go to the France after all, I thought, foreseeing a dreadful summer at home with hounds leaving and the Days leaving, and a terrible auction and then new people moving into Long Chill Farm.

Ten minutes or more passed and Valentine looked at her watch and said: "Hadn't you better get Dusty ready, Kate? It's a quarter to two and your class is the first after the interval, isn't it?"

Kate muttered "Yes," and we stood up and wandered across to the horses. Since Andrew's announcement, we had all lost interest in the show and in the hunter trial events. Laurence, Andrew, Valentine and I watched Kate jump a faultless round in dismal silence. Even when she was announced the winner of the children's hunter trial class, not one of us could raise a cheer.

It was time then for most of us to mount for the pairs class and, as I tightened Daystar's girths, I decided that I hated hunter trials, and that I would never go near them again. Kate and I didn't even bother to practise together. We stood in the collecting ring in gloomy, hopeless silence, until the steward called our numbers. We rode forward then and the starter looked at me and said: "Don't go wrong this time," and I said: "No, I won't," and produced a grimace which was meant to be a smile. A few minutes later we had started. Our horses were close together and behind us echoed cries of good luck.

I can't remember much about our round. I hardly lived it. My mind was far away hunting over quite a different landscape. My eye was seeing a familiar kennel yard, lit by moonlight, dim at dusk, sparkling amid the rays of an early sun; dingy, but somehow beautiful, beneath a fall of snow. But in spite of that Kate and I seemed fated to remain together. Perhaps our horses realised the state of our minds and preferred to stay close to one another, or perhaps we rode better because we weren't bothering about lengthening strides or trying to take off in special places. Whatever it was, we jumped a better round as a pair than we had ever jumped before. We knew it long before we reached the finishing post and heard the appreciative burst of clapping from the crowd.

We dismounted and patted Dusty and Daystar for ages and gave them pony nuts out of our pockets.

Mr. Day came across and said: "There's several people interested in the horses. A big dealer from the Midlands in particular. He's coming over tomorrow to talk business. I didn't like to fix up anything without consulting you and the rest first."

Kate seemed to stop breathing for a moment. A ghastly silence fell.

"You kept wonderfully together," said Mr. Day at last, turning to me. "I should think you're the winners all right."

"I doubt it," I said.

The afternoon was fast becoming evening. Most of the spectators were having tea. I thought of a large horse dealer with a walking stick looking at the Days' horses on the morrow.

"First in the pair class," announced the microphone, "Numbers twenty-five and twenty-nine, Second, twenty-seven and twenty-eight." I missed the rest.

"There, what did I say?" cried Mr. Day.

"Valentine and Andrew are second," said Kate mounting.

We cantered across to the judges' wagon and it was wonderful to know that Andrew and Valentine were the pair behind us. In the ring the band was playing a march. If only the future was free of calamity, I thought . . . If only the owners of Long Chill Farm had never decided to sell, this would have been an historic moment for us, a new triumph to add to the annals of the Chill Valley Hunt. But with no hunt there can be no annals, and no one will want to celebrate tonight.

"Pity you went wrong in the first class," said the Master of the East Nightley, who seemed to be judging the hunter trial events as well as the hunter class, as he handed me my rosette. "Your mare was going so well."

"I know, I'm afraid I was an awful fool," I said.

We all cantered back to the collecting ring together, and Andrew said: "What a triumph," but not as though he meant it.

"It's five o'clock," said Valentine.

"And time for home," added Andrew. "I wonder where Harry is."

"On his way," said Valentine, pointing to where she could see him in the distance.

We tied our rosettes to our horses' bridles, and Laurence said: "We've each got a red one, aren't we lucky?"

Valentine and Andrew and Kate made no answer. I muttered: "Yes."

"Jolly good," called Harry, drawing near. "Look, I've got a red one too," he continued. "Everyone else in my class had three refusals. So, although I had eighteen faults I was still first."

"Jolly good," said Kate.

"That's fine," said Andrew. Laurence and I added our compliments.

"And now home," said Andrew again. "And let's go quickly. I couldn't bear any more congratulations."

"Same here," said Valentine.

We rode away from the show ground without even saying good-bye to our parents. Behind us, the band was playing again. In the main ring the open jumping had just begun.

"We should be home by half-past eight at the latest," said Laurence.

"If we don't get lost," said Kate.

Lympton looked deserted. "I expect they're all at the show," said Andrew.

We passed The Limes. The fantail pigeons were

fluttering on the grass in the stable yard; otherwise, there was no sign of life. We found the lane we had missed the day before. The nut grove was green and golden in the sunlight. We cantered along the Roman road, and trotted through a wood carpeted with bluebells. Birds were singing quietly, as they do in the evening; the hedges and banks were bright with flowers. The whole world seemed to be ours as we rode beneath the sun and the cloudless blue of the sky. We saw no one but a distant tractor driver, and a man and his dog driving cows across green pastures. But even such a lovely evening could not dispel our gloomy thoughts and we rode, with one accord, in dismal silence. At last we saw Chidlington before us, and we came to the hill where we had lunched the day before. From then on, the countryside was familiar to all of us, and we rode tortured by memories of days we could never hope to live again. Allate looked lovelier to us than it had ever looked before. Cricketers were playing in white flannels on a green dappled by sunlight. The trees were part gold, part green, and beyond the church the sun was setting.

We took the old familiar track which would lead us down into the valley, and on each side of us, the bracken was thick and green and the gorse bright with flower. There was the smell of pine cones, and the ground was soft beneath our horses' hoofs. I think all of us, except perhaps Harry, had hounds with us, at that moment, in our imagination. I know I heard the horn calling "home" across the silent valley and thought of Bert Saunders waiting for us in the kennel yard, grumbling but kind at heart, as of old. We came to the valley. On the pond in front of the farmhouse the ducks were having their last paddle before bed. In the stable yard Nesta was basking in the rays from the setting sun. The hounds heard us and started to sing; the terriers joined in with their high-pitched yapping voices and the combination was deafening.

"Do you mind if we go home now and come down later to make the puddings?" Laurence shouted to the Days. "I don't think we ought to keep Overture and Daystar hanging about."

"Yes, of course," said Andrew. "Anything you like."

Because there seemed nothing left to say, Laurence and I rode home in silence. We put out horses away and gave them substantial feeds, and large bulging nets of hay, and clean water.

Neither of us wanted to go indoors to dinner. We weren't hungry, and we knew there would be a large hotpot waiting for us, and that Mummy would be upset if we didn't eat at least two-thirds of it. We dawdled outside for ages and when we eventually did go indoors, we were haunted by remorse, because our parents had waited for us. We forced soup down our throats and drank the wine Daddy had opened to celebrate us winning two first prizes.

But, though we tried to be cheerful, we were obviously gloomy, and Mummy and Daddy were perplexed by our mood. For some reason, neither Laurence nor I could bear to tell them the reason for our misery and we felt meaner and more horrible each moment.

At last, dinner was over and Laurence and I wandered out into the garden and stood and gazed at our horses over their box doors.

"We'd better go down soon," said Laurence, after some time had passed. "We *did* say we'd make the puddings."

"I wish we hadn't," I said, seeing the Days in a mood ten times worse than our own.

"Soon it'll be dark," said Laurence.

"I know," I answered, thinking that if we stayed at Little Hall long enough the Days would have made the puddings by the time we reached Long Chill Farm. Then we heard the back door open and we both jumped guiltily for no reason at all.

"Telephone," called Mummy into the gathering dusk. "Telephone."

Wild possibilities rushed into my mind. This is it, I thought, though what *it* was, beyond being wonderful news, I had no idea.

"You go," said Laurence.

"It's your turn," I shouted, already running towards the house.

"It's David Peterborough for you, Sandy," said Mummy as I reached the kitchen.

All my hopes fell in one appalling crash. I was so certain by then that the call was from Kate, that in a matter of seconds I should be hearing her saying: "It's all right. Everything's all right."

"What's the matter, Sandy? You've gone quite white," asked Mummy anxiously.

"I expect he wants to know how we did," I said, walking slowly towards the hall.

I picked up the receiver and David Peterborough said: "Hallo, is that you, Sandy?"

I said: "Yes," and he inquired how we had done

during the day. I told him without much enthusiasm, though I tried to sound cheerful.

"Well, I've got some news for you," said David Peterborough, in a kind uncle-ish sort of voice, when I had finished. "I've bought Long Chill Farm, and the Days and the Hunt and the kennels can all stay."

The room seemed to whirl round me and, for a moment, I thought I was going to fall. Then, instead of speaking to David Peterborough, I yelled: "Laurence, Laurence, quick, quick," as loudly as I could. There was a sound of running feet, and I heard Daddy call: "What's happening?" before I remembered that I still had the receiver in my hand. "Thanks terribly," I shrieked down it. "I think it's too wonderful for words. Thank you, thank you so much."

I told David Peterborough then how everything had been working up to an awful climax—how the Days' horses were to have been sold on the morrow, how the Days themselves were nearly attached to jobs miles away, and how by Saturday there would have been an advertisement for our hounds in *Horse and Hound*, and most of all I told him of the terrible gloom which had been hanging over us for weeks and weeks. Then I thanked him all over again.

David Peterborough laughed and said: "Not at all," and "Please don't mention it. I've always wanted to take my money out of stocks and shares and put it into land and you've made me take the plunge at last, for which I am truly grateful." He told me that he had meant to leave buying the farm until the day of the auction, but when we had had tea with him he had realised that by then it might be too late. "That's why I rushed up to London today," he continued, "and missed seeing you compete. Tomorrow I hope to come over and really look at the land I've bought, before leaving for France."

Laurence was beside me, listening.

"It's all right. Everything's all right," I said to him.

Already I was making plans for the future, seeing our first cub-hunting meet, with the dew still on the grass, seeing another ball, and a Chill Valley point-to-point.

"You'll let the Days know, won't you?" asked David Peterborough. "I'll be down to see you all and talk business with Mr. Day at about eleven in the morning, if that's all right."

"I'm sure it will be," I said, beginning to say thank you all over again.

A few seconds later. David Peterborough rang off.

"Oh, isn't it wonderful? He's bought Long Chill Farm and everything can stay just as it is," I cried, turning to Laurence. I felt as though I had wakened from a long and terrible nightmare and realised that I had dreamed it all.

"I always knew something would turn up," said Laurence, laughing.

We told our parents the news and then we tore out of the house and across the lawn and down into the sunlit valley. I felt as though I could run for ever. I could only think, it's true, it's true. Our hunt is saved. In my imagination I saw our young hounds hunting, and a mellow autumn, with early mornings spent in the saddle and evenings when we boned our boots and brushed and sponged our coats and breeches. All the work which had seemed so tiresome once, now appeared quite differently to me.

We found the Days arguing in the dining-room. I was suddenly struck dumb, and Laurence broke the news. When he had stopped speaking they stood and stared at us for a moment as though the impossible had happened, and then they all began to shriek at once.

"Really? Honestly?" cried Andrew.

"Oh, oh, how wonderful!" cried Kate. "I can't believe it."

"I'm going to tell Mum and Dad," said Valentine, hastening from the room.

"I'm going to tell Harry. He's in bed," cried Kate, rushing after Valentine and thundering upstairs.

"How did he know about the auction and everything?" asked Andrew.

"I told him," I said, "when we had tea together in The Country Kitchen. And you put the wind up him when we all had tea at The Limes, that's why he didn't wait until the auction."

"It's wonderful, really," said Andrew, as though he still couldn't believe the news was true.

"You know if we hadn't held the Chill Valley Hunter Trials, and those women hadn't been so beastly, it could never have happened," said Laurence. "Because Sandy would never have had tea with David Peterborough and told him about the auction."

"Well, that means the ball's really responsible," said Andrew. "Because if she hadn't gone into Chidlington to have her hair done she wouldn't have met David Peterborough and have had tea with him."

"In fact, it is really our attempt to raise five thousand

pounds which has saved everything," said Laurence, unable to keep a note of triumph from his voice.

"You sound as though you're playing the unwinding game," I said.

"Hallo," shrieked Harry, dashing into the room in his pyjamas. "Isn't it absolutely fantastic?"

Kate followed with a pile of cassettes. "I feel quite weak with relief," she cried.

"We've still got to make the pudding," said Andrew, eyeing the cassettes.

"I know, but we must play something first," cried Kate.

Mr. and Mrs. Day had entered the room. "What's this about the Honourable David Peterborough buying the farm and us stopping?" asked Mr. Day, glaring at me in the most frightening way.

It was some minutes before Laurence and I persuaded Mr. Day to believe our story. Then he rushed away to fetch drinks and the rest of us danced round the table like maniacs, shrieking "*A hunting we will go*" and singing *John Peel*.

Mr. Day returned with a tray loaded with glasses, and we all drank sherry and cider.

Much later, we wandered over to the boiler house, and stirred the puddings, and mixed oatmeal with the meat already cooked. We became filled with a calm content then. We planned the future and the moon came out and turned the valley silver.

"I feel as though I've been retrieved from death," said Kate.

"It'll be marvellous to wake up tomorrow and know that we're here for ages; that we needn't leave unless we want to; that the nightmare's over," said Valentine.

"It's just unbelievably wonderful," said Andrew in a dreamy voice, gazing beyond the farm, to where the moon was shining amid stars, above Badgers Copse.

And so you must leave us all dreaming together of the days to come, forgetting the puddings stewing in the coppers, seeing only our hounds running in full cry across the valley—Viking, Verger, Vagabond and Venus, close to the rest—hearing the gone away; feeling our horses beneath us, a breeze in our faces; and in front the old, familiar landscape so charged with memory for us all.

THE END

www.boarding.org